FORMULA ONE
THE RIVALS

FORMULA ONE

TONY DODGINS

THE RIVALS

F1'S GREATEST DUELS

IVY PRESS

Contents

Previous page Nigel Mansell and Nelson Piquet crash in the 1988 Japanese GP at Suzuka.

Opposite Mercedes pair Lewis Hamilton (44) and Nico Rosberg fight into the uphill first turn of the 2015 US GP at Circuit Of The Americas, Austin, Texas.

Foreword
by Mark Webber

I think it was Michael Jordan who said it: "I've failed over and over again in my life. And that is why I succeed."

It's the thing about sports people that should not be underestimated. A consummate, elegant performer like a Roger Federer can make it look easy. But it's not. Hard work will always trump talent that doesn't work hard.

In motor racing, that's especially true. My partner Ann and I know that only too well. The driving is only part of it and there are many more downs than ups. That's why I called my autobiography *Aussie Grit: My Formula One Journey*.

Journey is what it is, and there are no guarantees that you will reach your personal destination. If you are fortunate enough to reach the pinnacle, Formula 1, and get your backside into a car capable of winning races and championships, the stakes are raised tenfold. There is always a talented individual in the other car.

Rivalries are the lifeblood of all sport. As a teenager, I was absorbed by the Ayrton Senna and Alain Prost McLaren days. It's true what they say: the expression 'teammate' is a misnomer. You can have healthy rivalries with drivers from other teams. At Red Bull, I had great fights with World Champions like Lewis Hamilton at McLaren, Jenson Button at Brawn, and Fernando Alonso, then driving for Ferrari. But it's the guy on the other side of the garage, in my case Sebastian Vettel, who you are ultimately measured against. He can be more mortal enemy than 'mate'. He's the one whose times you first look for, whose set-up you want to understand.

Formula 1 can be a brutal environment. It's a team sport, yes, but it's you individually being measured against the stopwatch every couple of weeks, with no place to hide.

In my early F1 days I had some great highlights, such as finishing fifth in Paul Stoddart's Minardi at my home grand prix in 2002, scoring the team's first points. And achieving Jaguar's only front row start at Malaysia in 2004. But it took me seven years to get myself into a car that allowed me to aim for the top step of the podium – and to truly understand rivalry.

As luck would have it, I broke my leg just as it happened, but I became an F1 winner at Nurburgring in 2009. By 2010, I really felt ready to challenge for the championship. I was so stoked by my first win that year, in Barcelona, that I threw my helmet into the crowd! Seb and I are fine now, but we certainly had our moments that year. There was Turkey, and Silverstone, but also some of my greatest memories, like winning Monaco and that infamous British Grand Prix. It's like the American gymnast Mary Lou Retton said: "A trophy carries dust, but memories last forever."

I'm a big believer in that, and my hope is that memories of some of the greatest rivalries in our sport – which I feel privileged to be part of – will be rekindled by the words and glorious pictures in this book.

Introduction

Performing at the very top level of any activity takes immense commitment, dedication and sacrifice.

It's a tough enough challenge for sportsmen to extract the maximum from themselves, especially over a sustained period. But throw in a competitive situation that becomes personal and which can threaten professional shelf life, and it's a different level again. Rivalries are the lifeblood of sport. They become defining – and enduring. Whether it's Muhammad Ali and Joe Frazier, Rafael Nadal and Roger Federer or Ayrton Senna and Alain Prost, great rivalries transcend their sport.

The idea of looking back over F1 history and exploring some of the most memorable, was highly appealing. As a 15-year-old, I was a Niki Lauda fan totally absorbed by the battle with James Hunt for the 1976 World Championship.

Don't ask me why I was a Lauda fan. Maybe it was because he drove for Ferrari and Ferrari road cars were things of beauty that made you stop and stare. Maybe it was because he took 18 pole positions over two years in 1974–5, so seemed to be the out-and-out quickest. The calculating, consistent, computer-driver tags came further down the road.

Whatever it was, I couldn't care less that James was British. It became completely engrossing: the disqualifications, reinstatements, controversy, Niki's 1976 Nürburgring accident, the recovery, politics, the Fuji showdown, Niki's withdrawal and James's 11th-hour success. It was the year that took motor racing from the back pages of newspapers to the front. It was box office from first to last, even if it took another 37 years for the movie makers to get around to it with *Rush*!

James and Niki got along, and it stayed like that. But sometimes the intensity is just too much. More often than not, animosity creeps in when the rivals are in the same team: Gilles Villeneuve and Didier Pironi; Nelson Piquet and Nigel Mansell; Ayrton Senna and Alain Prost; Fernando Alonso and Lewis Hamilton; Lewis Hamilton and Nico Rosberg or Sebastian Vettel and Mark Webber.

It's one thing when a race crew is battling a rival team, but quite another when the chief opponent comes from within. Team personnel are split, paranoia sets in, and all occurring amid the tiring, high-pressure environment of a global travelling circus. It's not surprising that those situations can implode spectacularly, none more so than at McLaren in 2007 with Alonso and a first-year Hamilton. That year itself deserves its own book!

In the beginning, motor racing was populated by well-heeled 'gentleman racers'. Stirling Moss is widely regarded as the first 'professional' racing driver, which attracted some derisory comment from Mike Hawthorn, his rival for the 1958 World Championship. But the spirit of sportsmanship was still well to the fore, even if anyone tasked with overtaking Nino Farina might have disagreed …

Moss's actions in supporting Hawthorn against a disqualification at the end of 1958 helped ensure that Stirling would go down in history as the best driver never to win a World Championship, even if Moss himself blames the misinterpretation of a pit signal and his own failure to chase a fastest lap point. I'd like to think that such sportsmanship still exists, and the Hamilton family made a good show of it, congratulating Max Verstappen in the aftermath of the controversial Abu Dhabi race in 2021.

Another rivalry which became the subject of a docufilm is that between Gilles Villeneuve and Didier Pironi at the beginning of the 1980s. Rivalry, actually, is probably a misnomer. In terms of speed, Didier was never really a threat to Gilles, but after a season with a somewhat agricultural chassis in the early days of F1's first turbo era, they suddenly found themselves with a championship-winning car on their hands, and Didier was getting closer.

Suddenly, it mattered. There was Fédération Internationale du Sport Automobile (FISA) and Formula One Constructors' Association (FOCA) politicking in the background, which meant that Imola '82 was an unusual race boycotted by the FOCA teams. Pironi speaks of a pre-race agreement between the Ferrari and Renault drivers to put on a show for the crowd in the first half, then restore themselves to grid order at half distance and begin the race proper. According to him, their teams didn't know.

Villeneuve was adamant that there were team orders and that Pironi stole the race from him. Pironi says there were none. Previously, there had been no turbulence in the relationship, but Villeneuve was adamant he would not speak to Pironi again. Determined to beat Didier's time on his last qualifying run at the next race at Zolder in Belgium, Villeneuve crashed fatally after colliding with Jochen Mass. Rather than a rivalry, it was more accurately a one-race spat with tragic consequences. But Villeneuve's worldwide following, their personalities and personal circumstances made it much more than that.

Villeneuve was the fastest man of his generation and the man who succeeded him was Alain Prost. While Villeneuve was sideways and spectacular, Alain was the polar opposite; his car seldom out of line. He didn't look fast, but the watch told a different story. He became France's first World Champion in 1985 and very much the main man at McLaren – until Ayrton Senna arrived.

Team co-ordinator Jo Ramirez tells how Senna was obsessed with Prost from day one. Ayrton knew he was quicker and didn't want to just beat Prost: he wanted to humiliate him. So superior was the McLaren MP4/4 in 1988 that they had no rivals.

Senna won his first championship in that '88 season together, and they rubbed along just about okay, but any relationship disintegrated the following season. Prost regained the championship after a low-speed contact between the pair at Suzuka's chicane. The record books would say one championship apiece at McLaren. That stuck in Senna's craw after he'd suffered numerous reliability issues, allied to the fact that Prost was on his way out of there, to Ferrari.

A year on it was déjà vu, with Senna bundling Prost's Ferrari off the road at Suzuka's first corner to clinch a second world title. No matter that it happened at 150mph. For Ayrton, it was an eye for an eye. The needle lasted right up until Prost chose to retire in 1993 rather than go head-to-head in the same team as Senna again at Williams in 1994. A rapprochement was just underway when Senna died at Imola in May.

Ayrton's death robbed the sport of a much-anticipated rivalry between its established star, who many believe to be the greatest ever, and an up-and-coming Michael Schumacher. Michael took over as the man to beat. After a season of intrigue, politics, disqualifications and drama that was almost a match for '76, Damon Hill nearly achieved that feat, only losing out at the final round in Adelaide when Schumacher turned in on him and took both of them out of the race.

Then there is the case of an established star being challenged by a driver with a lesser reputation. Such was the case when Nelson Piquet left Brabham for a dominant Williams-Honda in 1986. Frank Williams had signed Nigel Mansell as a strong number two to Keke Rosberg, with nothing in Nigel's four years at Lotus indicating that he was a future World Champion.

But already in his first season at Williams, Mansell looked good, often matching Rosberg and winning his first Grand Prix at Brands Hatch towards the end of the year, then another at Kyalami. Piquet had a rude awakening and Mansell, by rights, deserved to win the title, until heartbreakingly robbed by an exploding Goodyear tyre within touching distance of his goal in the Adelaide season finale. He would achieve his life's ambition, but it would take another six years.

Michael Schumacher and Mika Häkkinen first crossed swords almost a decade before they found themselves fighting out F1 World Championships. That was at Macau, in Formula 3, when a rude chop decided the issue in Michael's favour when Mika had it in the bag.

Häkkinen, as calm and phlegmatic as they come, stored it in the memory bank. By 1998, Schumacher was into his third season with Ferrari after his move from Benetton and still chasing a first world title with Maranello. He'd got close in '97, losing out in the final round at Jerez after a cack-handed collision with Jacques Villeneuve decided the championship in the French-Canadian's favour.

But, for the first time in his F1 career, which began in '91, Häkkinen had a car worthy of him. Again, it went down to the wire

in '98 and, again, Schumacher lost out. In '99, Häkkinen beat him again to clinch back-to-back titles.

Mika was more notable for what he didn't say than what he did. In Malaysia '99, when Schumacher returned after breaking a leg at Silverstone, it was Ferrari teammate Eddie Irvine who was battling Häkkinen for the championship. After taking pole position, Schumacher led but let Irvine through, proceeding to mess Häkkinen around for the rest of the afternoon, being slow to pick up the throttle on corners, then bolting when the pit stops were due, only to slow down again once Häkkinen was back on his tail. "He's the best number two in the world as well as the best number one", Irvine said.

Some of it was all a bit marginal but, when asked, Häkkinen refused to be drawn, gave his wan smile, and then drove brilliantly to clinch his second title in Japan. When Schumacher rudely chopped Mika at Spa in 2000, he responded with one of F1's most memorable overtakes and then, post-race, quietly made his opinion known to Michael, and only Michael, with a few quiet words. No histrionics. There was genuine respect between the pair and never any trash-talking.

In 2021, F1 fans were treated to a very special rivalry. It's rare that two true superstars find themselves with competitive, potentially championship-winning machinery in different teams in the same year. But that's what happened with seven-time World Champion Lewis Hamilton at Mercedes and Max Verstappen at Red Bull.

In some ways, it reminded you of the way Senna dealt with Prost, albeit that Verstappen and Hamilton were in different teams.

Verstappen was uncompromising in his approach, more than once giving Hamilton a 'back off or crash' option on early-season opening laps.

It's probably fair to say that for the first half of the season, Verstappen had a slight car advantage but that the pendulum swung after a significant mid-season Mercedes car upgrade. Red Bull team principal Christian Horner speaks of brilliant drives from Verstappen in Mexico and Austin keeping him in it.

Two of the greatest drivers ever, in two absolutely top-notch teams, provided compelling sport for the entire season.

The manner in which it was decided in Abu Dhabi was a travesty even if, on the balance of the year, Verstappen deserved his championship. But for pure drama, did their rivalry surpass that of '76?

Over the years, it has been a privilege to work in what is such an absorbing environment and witness some of these top performers in the pursuit of their dreams and ambitions. I can only scratch the surface, but I hope that in the following pages I can offer at least some insight into the battles and personalities to have graced this fantastic sport.

Fangio vs. Ascari

Fangio
24 Grand Prix wins
5 Championships

Ascari
13 Grand Prix wins
2 Championships

It's difficult to put into perspective the achievements of Juan Manuel Fangio in comparison to drivers of the modern era. Michael Schumacher and Lewis Hamilton have each won seven World Championships, but each driving for just two teams. Hamilton started racing F1 machinery at 22, Schumacher also got his first drive, for the Jordan team, at 22 – Juan Manuel was almost 39 when he lined up for his debut 1950 British Grand Prix in an Alfa Romeo.

Fangio, universally known as 'the Maestro', would go on to win five World Championships between 1950 and 1957, driving for Alfa Romeo, Mercedes, Ferrari and Maserati. It was a feat that remained unsurpassed for almost half a century before Michael Schumacher claimed his sixth title in 2003.

The son of an Italian immigrant family, he was born on 24 June 1911 and raised in Balcarce, Argentina, working in a garage from a young age to bolster the family income. After stunning success in South America he arrived on the European racing scene in 1948, his performances earning him a seat with the Alfa Romeo works team for 1950, the very first season of the Formula 1 World Championship.

When Fangio joined Alfa, its established star was the fast but accident-prone Dr Giuseppe 'Nino' Farina, who had driven for them since before the Second World War. Farina had a reputation for being aloof, arrogant and difficult to pass in races if he put his mind to it, and he regularly put his mind to it.

In that inaugural World Championship, points were awarded 8-6-4-3-2 to the first five finishers, plus an additional point for fastest lap, and only a driver's best four finishes counted. The world title was effectively contested over six races; at Silverstone, Monaco, Bremgarten (Switzerland), Spa, Reims and Monza.

As the mighty Alfas took a clean sweep of all six races, Farina won in Britain, Switzerland and Italy, while Fangio took Monaco, Belgium and France – though it was Fangio who scored four pole positions to Farina's two. Farina's fourth place result at Spa proved decisive as Fangio suffered three retirements and only had his three wins to post. Thus, the inaugural World Champion title went to the Italian, 30 points to 27. Still, Fangio had established himself as the quicker driver in the team, much to Farina's chagrin. The following year the Italian could only finish fourth and his last full season of races was 1953. Farina's 1954 season was cut short by a crash in the Mille Miglia road race, compounded by burns to his legs he suffered at the Italian Grand Prix at Monza.

It was ironic that a survivor of the racing scene from the 1930s and 1940s, when drivers raced with no seat belts and a cloth helmet, should be killed driving his Lotus Cortina to the 1966 French Grand Prix.

"I was not surprised when I heard he died in a road accident, only that it didn't happen earlier ..." Fangio said. "I hated having to drive with him on the way to a race."

With Farina eclipsed at Alfa Romeo, Fangio's real rivalry would be with Alberto Ascari, star of the up-and-coming Scuderia Ferrari team. Ascari's father, Antonio, had been a national sporting figure, one of the greatest drivers of the 1920s before losing his life driving for Alfa Romeo in the French GP at Montlhéry, south of Paris. Alberto was just seven when his father died. Despite his grief, the accident did nothing to dampen Alberto's desire to follow in his father's footsteps. At 22 he drove a Ferrari sportscar in the 1940 Mille Miglia, a race he came to despise for its inherent danger to both competitors

and spectators. Ascari, partnered by his cousin Giovanni Minozzi, led before retiring, hugely impressing racing's aficionados. However, the Second World War interrupted his ambitions.

Alberto's mother, a racing widow, hoped that would be the end of it, but Ascari's close friend Luigi Villoresi persuaded him to get back behind the wheel once hostilities were over. Both drove for the works Maserati team and Ascari's obvious ability persuaded Enzo Ferrari that he should be signed for the team.

Alberto finished fifth in the 1950 World Championship. The Ferrari was unable to fight the dominant Alfa Romeos but the Scuderia was getting stronger and stronger. It was a great era for Italian machinery, with Fangio, Farina and Luigi Fagioli flying the Alfa flag against Ascari, Villoresi and Froilán González, who claimed Ferrari's first GP win at Silverstone in 1951 before moving on to the Maserati team, another great Italian marque.

But it was Fangio and Ascari who emerged as the clear No.1s in their respective teams. Fangio took the first of his five championships in 1951, by 31 points to 25 with wins in Switzerland, France and Spain, while Ascari won races in Germany and Italy. The German race, at Nürburgring, witnessed a great duel between the pair. Ascari took pole position and Fangio was aware that his thirsty Alfa would likely require a second fuel stop in the race. As Fangio led initially, Ascari took over as his rival pitted for the first time. The Argentine retook the lead just after half distance as Ascari made his lone pit stop, but Juan Manuel couldn't eke out a big enough advantage, and when he stopped again the race was lost to the Ferrari.

This burgeoning rivalry was temporarily extinguished by a change to F1's engine regulations for 1952, with races run to the

two-litre Formula 2. Without a suitable engine, Alfa Romeo withdrew from Formula 1, leaving the defending World Champion without a car. Farina jumped ship to partner Ascari at Ferrari, while Fangio didn't take part in an F1 race until June, when he drove non-championship races for BRM (British Racing Motors) at Albi in France and Dundrod in Northern Ireland.

He was due to drive a Maserati in a non-championship race at Monza the day after the Irish race but missed his connecting flight. He elected to drive through the night on mountain roads across the Alps and finally arrived at Monza half an hour before the race was due to start, absolutely shattered. Starting from the back of the grid, Fangio crashed out on the second lap and was thrown out as the car flipped into the trees. It was his closest brush with death in a long career of motor racing. He suffered multiple injuries, including a broken neck. Farina, who won the race, visited him in hospital in Milan and presented him with the victory garland. The chastened Maestro was forced to spend the rest of the year recuperating back in his native Argentina.

Of the seven grands prix in 1952, Alberto won six of them and was absent from the seventh, in Switzerland, after Enzo Ferrari sent him to compete at Indianapolis in a Ferrari 375, to no avail. Ascari won nine consecutive grands prix between Spa in June 1952 and the same race in 1953, his winning streak only halted by Mike Hawthorn's win for Ferrari at the French Grand Prix. It was a record unmatched until Sebastian Vettel steamrollered the second half of the 2013 season for Red Bull.

Back to full fitness for 1953, Fangio returned to the grid with Maserati and although Ascari and Ferrari dominated the year,

Opposite Juan Manuel Fangio stands between Alberto Ascari and Giuseppe Farina, who hold their trophies and bouquets after the British Grand Prix at Silverstone in 1950.

Left Ascari speeds past the pits on his way to another win and a second World Championship at Silverstone in 1953.

Below Three of the favourites line up for the '53 Italian GP – Ascari (4), Fangio (50) and Farina (6).

Above Fangio, Karl King (20) and Ascari prepare for the '54 French GP at Reims.

Right Portrait of Ascari at Monaco in '55, the race in which he vaulted into the harbour but was rescued, four days before dying while testing a Ferrari 750 Monza sportscar, at Monza.

Opposite Ascari at the wheel of the Lancia D50 at Monaco in '55.

there was an epic duel between the pair at Monza in the final race of the season. Ascari was already World Champion for the second time but surprised the paddock by announcing that he was leaving Ferrari for the new Lancia F1 team (yet another great Italian marque). Some say that a salary dispute was at the root of it; others put it down to an impending return by Mercedes and Ascari feeling that Lancia's new D50 might ultimately give him a better opportunity to take on the mighty German team. Also, the car's designer, Vittorio Jano, was behind the Alfa in which Alberto's father scored many of his greatest wins, and in which he also died.

Whatever, Ascari was determined to win in his Ferrari swansong. He was at his best leading from the front and less comfortable in a scrap, which is what many of the Monza slip-streamers turned into. Mike Hawthorn, who adored Ascari, believed him to be the fastest driver he'd ever seen and included Fangio in that assessment. The Maestro, however, would have taken issue with that. The pair shared the front row with Ascari's Ferrari teammate Farina at the 'Temple of Speed' that afternoon.

The trio broke away at the start, joined by Argentine Fangio protégé Onofre Marimón (killed at Nürburgring the following season) in a second Maserati. In an enthralling race, the lead changed hands multiple times, often each lap, until Marimón spun just after half distance at what was then the Curva Vedano, subsequently Parabolica and now the Curva Alboreto.

Legend has it that Fangio and Ascari could be seen looking over and grinning at each other as they blasted down the main straight. Starting the last lap, Fangio, Ascari and Farina were practically three abreast down the front straight. Ascari led from

Ferrari teammate Farina but there were no team orders and, just behind, were the Maseratis of Fangio and the lapped Marimón.

Into Vedano for the last time, Ascari passed one of the tail-enders but then slid sideways on oil, causing Farina to take evasive action and get on the grass. Fangio made it through on the inside but Marimón, trying to do the same, collected Ascari's Ferrari. The fans, expecting a four-car photo-finish, were greeted by a lone Fangio and so surprised was the man with the chequered flag, that he forgot to drop it. Some time later, Ascari and Marimón returned to the pits in a marshal's car, Onofre with a cut on his face and Alberto with a look of thunder on his …

In 1954, Fangio completed the first three races with Maserati before joining the returning Mercedes team for the remainder of the season and sweeping to his second world title with an impressive six victories in eight championship races. This time, it was Ascari's turn to be defending champion without a car. Lancia's D50 was not race-ready and he missed most of the year.

Although Lancia was technically in breach of contract, Ascari was honourable and loyal and only made a couple of one-off appearances with a Ferrari and a Maserati. When he'd signed with Lancia, he requested that the Mille Miglia be excluded from his racing schedule. But when teammate Luigi Villoresi hospitalized himself, Ascari changed his mind and came home first of the 378 starters in his Lancia D24. He won the race by more than half an hour!

When a couple of Lancia D50s finally did make it to the grid for the season finale at Pedralbes, Spain, in late October, a feisty Ascari took pole position more than a second quicker than Fangio's

Left When Fangio's Ferrari (22) broke, Stirling Moss's Maserati (36) won the 1956 Italian GP at Monza, 'the Maestro' taking over the car of Ferrari teammate Peter Collins (26) to share second place.

Opposite Fangio, Moss and Eugenio Castellotti take the start at Monaco in 1956.

Right Fangio next to girlfriend Andrea Berruet and a pensive-looking Peter Collins in the Principality.

Mercedes. In the race, he led convincingly and set the fastest lap before the clutch gave up. A degree of honour had been restored.

That finishing flourish continued into 1955 and the first race, the Argentine Grand Prix, held in January to allow cars to be shipped to South America. Ascari led in Fangio's backyard in Buenos Aires before spinning off on melting tar. Back in Europe Ascari easily won a couple of non-championship street races in Turin and Naples before the first European head-to-head with Mercedes at Monaco in May.

Around Monte Carlo, Ascari matched Fangio's pole time and split the Silver Arrows of the Maestro and his new Mercedes teammate Stirling Moss. He could not keep pace with the Mercedes pair in the race, however, with Moss almost a lap ahead of the Lancia when Fangio retired with a broken rear axle. But, on lap 81, with 19 to go, Stirling's engine failed and Ascari was left with a big lead, and failing brakes …

Lancia never had the opportunity to slow him down with a pitboard message because Ascari arrived at the harbour front chicane too quickly, threw the car sideways and went straight through the straw bales and into the harbour. The D50 sank like a stone and for what seemed like an eternity, there was no sign of its driver. But then Ascari's light blue helmet bobbed to the surface, and he swam towards a rescuing boat, having escaped with just a broken nose.

Ascari was a devoted family man but, all too aware of the potential consequences of racing, had cautioned his children, Antonio and Patrizia, about becoming too close to him. He was also deeply superstitious with a great respect of numerology –

the pseudoscientific belief in a divine or mystical relationship between a number and one or more coincidental events, often associated with the paranormal. Which made the circumstances of his death all the more strange.

Four days after the watery end to his Monaco GP, Ascari, on a whim, headed to Monza to watch Lancia's new star Eugenio Castellotti, whom he mentored, test a Ferrari sportscar. They had lunch together and then Ascari made a sudden decision to try the car himself, going out in his suit trousers and Castellotti's borrowed helmet.

After a couple of laps there was silence. Castellotti and fellow driver Luigi Villoresi went to investigate, only to find the remains of the shattered Ferrari at the Curva del Vialone (now the Ascari chicane). Ascari passed away before an ambulance could get to him.

No satisfactory explanation for the accident was ever produced. Theories ranged from delayed post-Monaco concussion causing a black-out, to swerving in avoidance of an errant labourer working on the track. Mike Hawthorn, meanwhile, suspected that tyres too wide for the car's rims may have been a factor.

What is certain is that Antonio and Alberto Ascari were both killed on the 26th of the month (July 1925 and May 1955 respectively) and both were aged 36. Both had amazing escapes four days before the accidents that took their lives, and both had taken to a circuit for the first time wearing borrowed crash helmets.

Ascari's funeral took place at the Piazza del Duomo in Milan. One million people paid their respects as the black coffin with Alberto's famous light blue helmet on top, went by. Fangio said, "I have lost my greatest opponent".

The great Argentine, now 44, had trained diligently to take on his younger rivals and won a tough opening race in 1955 in the blistering heat of Buenos Aires. The chassis of his Mercedes W196 heated up to such an extent that rubbing his right leg against it gave him burns which took a couple of months to heal, but he refused to stop.

Although Fangio won his third World Championship in 1955, the year was marred by the Le Mans disaster when a Mercedes sportscar was launched into the crowd. It resulted in Mercedes pulling out of the championship, interrupting the F1 careers of Fangio and teammate Stirling Moss, when they had been in a dominant position.

For 1956, Fangio moved to Ferrari and won his third consecutive title before switching back to Maserati in 1957 to claim his fourth successive title and his fifth overall. He started the year with a hat-trick of victories in Argentina, Monaco and France, but it is his majestic performance in winning the German GP at the Nürburgring, after a long pit stop delay, that remains one of the sport's enduring tales.

Having eyed up the hard compound tyres chosen by the Ferrari team for their drivers Mike Hawthorn and Peter Collins, Fangio guessed that they were going to run the whole race without a stop. He opted for a softer tyre with half his fuel on board, allowing him to run faster but necessitating a mid-race stop for more tyres and fuel. However, when he pitted from the lead, the mechanic removing the rear left wheel let the holding nut roll under the car. Locating it took nearly half a minute and Fangio's Maserati 250F left the pitlane in third place, 48 seconds behind Collins in second place,

with Hawthorn further up the road in the lead. Over the next 10 laps, Fangio broke and rebroke the lap record nine times passing Collins and squeaking past Hawthorn on what was F1's most challenging circuit. Hawthorn held on behind, but Fangio was still three seconds ahead at the flag.

"I have never driven that quickly in my life, and I don't want to again …" Fangio said, and he probably didn't. It would mark the final full season for the 46-year-old multiple World Champion. He would retire two races into the 1958 season with a fourth place finish at the French Grand Prix in Reims, nursing a Maserati which lost its clutch early in the race, Fangio timing his gear changes simply by listening to the engine note.

Stirling Moss said of him, "the best classroom of all time was probably two car lengths behind Juan Manuel Fangio." And that's only if you could get that close. Fangio brought a gravitas and sincerity to his profession that had a profound effect on all who raced with him. He was both competitive and generous, carefully shadowing Moss around Aintree when Stirling won the 1955 British Grand Prix, without the slightest hint that he had handed the race to his teammate on home soil.

Moss vs. Hawthorn

Moss
16 Grand Prix wins
0 Championships

Hawthorn
3 Grand Prix wins
1 Championship

At the end of 1957, after winning four successive World Championships, 'El Maestro' Juan Manuel Fangio found Maserati winding down its operation. At the age of 46, he would enter only selected races the following season as an independent. The 1958 season was thus the dawn of a new era, a year which witnessed both the first World Championship for manufacturers (constructors) and the first time that a Briton would realistically be a contender for the Drivers' Championship. But would it be Stirling Moss at Vanwall or Mike Hawthorn at Ferrari, or failing that, Hawthorn's teammate Peter Collins, a great friend of both men.

Moss, born 17 September 1929, had finished second to Fangio in the three previous championships, was acknowledged to be quicker than the Argentine great in a sportscar, and, in Britain, was already widely known as 'Mr Motor Racing'. If you upset the police by driving too quickly after UK speed limits were imposed, it was always, "Who do you think you are, Stirling Moss?" Among the GP fraternity Moss had already inherited Fangio's 'Maestro' tag.

Son of dentist Alfred Moss, Stirling had become the 'boy wonder' of British motorsport from 1948, competing in a 500cc Cooper that he bought himself at the tender age of 18. By mid-1951 he had scored over 30 wins, competing against the likes of Collins, who he would one day partner in Aston Martin sportscars. His father had wanted Stirling to become a dentist, and though happy to advise his son on business decisions, gave him no financial support for his early career.

His big break might have come in the 1952 season when on a visit to the factory in August 1951, Enzo Ferrari asked him to join the Scuderia as the third driver alongside Alberto Ascari and Luigi Villoresi for the following season. Ferrari would prepare a car for the non-championship race at Bari in September 1951. Intensely patriotic, Stirling turned the 1952 drive down, preferring to try and win in a British machine. However, he agreed to drive for Ferrari in the Bari race. Having journeyed all the way down to Bari on the Italian coast, he found that there had been a change of plan, for which he had not been informed, and Piero Taruffi would be driving 'his' car. No proper explanation was ever given to Moss for the abrupt rebuff from Modena, but he vowed never to drive for Ferrari again. To add insult to injury, Ascari won all six grands prix in 1952, while Moss, in a mixture of uncompetitive British cars, retired in every race he entered.

At the end of 1952, Enzo did manage to sign a British driver, the 23-year-old 'Farnham Flyer', Mike Hawthorn. 'Snowball' as he was sometimes known because of his shock of blond hair, had impressed in 1952 with drives in a Cooper-Bristol that netted him two fourth places and a podium at the British Grand Prix. The differences between Moss and Hawthorn were pronounced. Moss was short and meticulous in his attitude to racing; Hawthorn was 6' 2" and disdained the professional approach, preferring to cast himself in the role of gentleman racer. He could afford to. A family friend had bought him the Cooper-Bristol and it was entered by his father Leslie, a wealthy garage proprietor, who owned a Jaguar dealership, the Tourist Trophy Garage in Farnham, Surrey.

Partnering Alberto Ascari in 1953, Hawthorn made a name for himself when he won a fantastic race-long, wheel-to-wheel tussle with Fangio's Maserati in the French Grand Prix at Reims. It became known as 'The Race of the Century' and placed Hawthorn in the record books as the first British driver, indeed, the first driver other than Italians or Argentines to win a *grande épreuve* Formula 1 race. He had beaten the boy wonder to a statistic that looked destined to come Stirling's way.

"I was conscious of the media fanning the flames of our rivalry," Moss said at the time and on the surface it looked as though the two rivals were the best of chums, laughing and joking together in the pits or chatting together on the grid whenever the cameras were around. In private it was a wholly different matter. Hawthorn, alluding to Moss's Jewish heritage, called him 'Moses' and confessed to friends that he really didn't like Stirling Moss. At the root of it, barring the casual anti-Semitism, was a scorn for Stirling's professional attitude to the sport, and the fact that he was racing cars for a living. Hawthorn could rely on income from a garage business built up by his father. It was an era when the word 'amateur' had cachet among the upper classes and was yet to be widely used in the context of bungling and second-rate.

Hawthorn got the better of Moss in 1954, continuing with Ferrari alongside Froilán Gonzáles and ending the year with a win in the Spanish Grand Prix at Barcelona and third place in the Drivers' Championship. Moss had been forced to buy his own Maserati 250F after the team had signed up its drivers and finished the season with a solitary third place at Spa.

In 1955 the rivals' fortunes were completely reversed. Long-time Mercedes team manager Alfred Neubauer, a giant of the sport in more ways than one – and the man who had guided Richard Seaman though his time at the Silver Arrows in the 1930s – needed a competent back-up for his No.1 driver Fangio.

In the days when cars could be handed over to teammates mid-race, it was important that the No.2 was in contention with a donor car. Moss at Mercedes was the perfect fit. Here was a team that matched Stirling's perfectionism in preparation.

"It was an incredible company, particularly in those days," Stirling told journalist David Tremayne. "Neubauer had a terrific sense of humour and he was a man that you felt was almost like a father figure."

Mercedes' dominance of the 1955 season was akin to their superiority in the hybrid engine era from 2014. Fangio strolled to the title with Moss following close behind, winning his first British Grand Prix at Aintree along the way. It was a season already tinged with tragedy, one in which both Hawthorn and the Mercedes team were both involved.

Early in the Le Mans 24-hour race, Hawthorn, driving for Jaguar, had overtaken Lance Macklin's Austin-Healey at the start of the pits straight, then made a sudden dart to the right for the pits. The Jaguar was equipped with new development disc brakes and Macklin was caught unawares by the deceleration. To miss the Jaguar, he swerved into the path of two rapidly closing Mercedes, driven by Pierre Levegh and the lead car of Fangio, who was sharing a Mercedes 300 SLR with Stirling Moss.

The hapless Levegh was unable to avoid the swerving Macklin, rode up over the back of the Healey and was launched over the low banking separating the track from the spectators, and into the crowd. In motor racing's greatest ever tragedy, Levegh and 83 spectators and officials were killed. More than seven hours later, after board directors had all been contacted in Stuttgart, Mercedes

Opposite Moss ready to start from the pole at Goodwood in '51.

Above Moss in his Cooper-Alta at the '53 French GP at Reims.

Left Hawthorn accepts the bubbly after winning the same race.

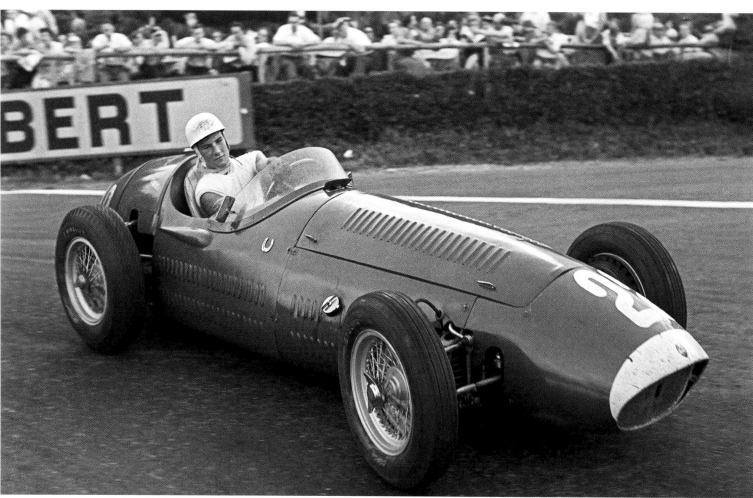

withdrew its other two cars. Team manager Neubauer suggested
that Jaguar might like to do likewise, but his invitation was declined
by team manager Frank 'Lofty' England, with Hawthorn and co-
driver Ivor Bueb going on to win.

Underneath a picture of Hawthorn drinking the victory
champagne, the French *L'Auto Journal* published a sarcastic
caption, 'À votre santé, Monsieur Hawthorn!' ('To your health,
cheers, Mr Hawthorn!').

Hawthorn had been horrified at what had happened.
Motorsport entrepreneur Rob Walker, who entered cars in both
F1 and sportscar events, said that after Ivor Bueb had taken over
the Jaguar, a highly emotional Hawthorn came over to him and
Macklin. He said the accident was all his fault and begged Macklin
to forgive him. Lois, wife of Tony Rolt (Le Mans winner with Jaguar in
1953) poured him a tumbler of brandy and told him to shut up. Then
Lofty England sat him down and convinced him that he was not to
blame, and the Hawthorn/Bueb D-type Jaguar raced on to victory.
Thereafter Mike always maintained it was not his fault.

The repercussions of Le Mans 1955 were enormous, including
temporary (and not so temporary), bans on motor racing in
France, Spain, Switzerland and West Germany. It also brought an
abrupt end to Moss's career with Mercedes, who pulled out of
all forms of motor racing at the end of the year – a year in which
Stirling claimed an epic victory in the Mille Miglia, with motor-
racing journalist and co-driver Denis Jenkinson. The irony was that
Hawthorn had sparked the accident that denied Moss his best
chance to win Le Mans (he never did) and then won himself –
at the same time losing Stirling a drive with a team he fitted like a

glove, and which looked destined to dominate the sport in
the years to come.

Fangio decamped to Ferrari for 1956 and became World
Champion for his third marque. Moss, no longer in 'the Maestro's'
shadow, signed a contract as official No.1 driver for Maserati,
who paid him £500 per race for all rounds of the championship.
He was also free to drive elsewhere in races that Maserati was not
contesting, hence Stirling winning the Silverstone International
Trophy non-championship race in a Vanwall, for which British
industrialist team owner Tony Vandervell paid him the princely
sum of £1,500 – a very healthy payday in 1956.

Moss had always wanted to drive a British car in Formula 1
and knew that Vandervell was serious about his motor racing.
He therefore accepted an offer to drive the Vanwalls, resplendent
in British racing green colours in 1957. Despite a few reservations
about reliability, he managed to win the British, Pescara and Italian
Grands Prix en route to second in the championship behind that
man Fangio again, who displayed all his craft to win his fifth title
for his fourth marque.

Hawthorn, meanwhile, had not added to his victory tally since
the Spanish Grand Prix of 1954 and it's probably fair to say that the
majority of British racing fans were in the Moss camp for the 1958
season. The Vanwalls looked like being able to offer up a feasible
challenge to the continental opposition for the first time on the back
of Stirling's win with a 'macchina Inglese' at Monza, the shrine of
Italian motor racing.

Moss, by now, was on £1,000 for each grand prix with Vanwall,
and also had contracts for selected sportscar races with Maserati

and Aston Martin, as well as the freedom to race Rob Walker's Coopers in F1 and F2 when Vanwall did not require his services. Moss really valued his association with Walker (part of the Johnnie Walker whisky dynasty), a self-effacing man with impeccable manners, whose passport once listed his occupation as 'gentleman'. Stirling always claimed that he and Walker never had a written contract, but long before Bernie Ecclestone began collective bargaining on behalf of racing teams in the 1970s, Walker was astute enough to ensure that race organizers had to meet his financial terms if they wanted Moss gracing their starting grids!

With Vanwall not quite ready for new F1 regulations in 1958, it was aboard a Walker Cooper-Climax adapted from an F2 car that Moss won the first round of the championship in January, famously beating the more powerful Maseratis and Ferraris over 80 laps of Buenos Aires. All weekend Moss duped everyone into thinking he would have to make a three-minute pit stop with the Cooper (the wheels of which had four-stud fixings rather than the traditional F1 'knock-off' spinners) because Dunlop had advised that in the gruelling heat the tyres would only last 30–40 laps. The two-litre, four-cylinder Climax engine was capable of going through without refuelling, however, and Moss did just that, finishing with exposed, flapping tyre canvases on the little car. By the time that Ferrari had realized what the game was and sent Luigi Musso after him, it was too late, Moss taking the chequered flag 2.7 seconds to the good with Hawthorn third. It was a historic moment for F1 – the first Grand Prix win for both Cooper and a rear-engined car.

With four months before round two in Monaco, Vanwall's car was now ready, but Moss had a problematic weekend with

reliability at a circuit on which he excelled and retired, as did Hawthorn, after both had led the race. Stirling made amends to win the Dutch Grand Prix at Zandvoort, lapping Hawthorn en route as Mike struggled with an ill-handling Ferrari. At Spa, Moss suffered one of the biggest disappointments of his career when he made a great start, had a comfortable lead by the end of the opening lap and then missed his shift from fourth to fifth, grenading his engine when he found himself in neutral as he went full back on the accelerator. Vanwall teammate Tony Brooks took the spoils ahead of pole man Hawthorn's Ferrari.

The French Grand Prix at Reims was totally dominated by Hawthorn, the Ferrari winning from pole position in a race that was marred by the fatal accident to teammate Luigi Musso. Moss, contending with gearbox problems, finished second. In much the same way that Hawthorn proved unbeatable in France, so did his Ferrari teammate and great friend Peter Collins in the British Grand Prix at Silverstone, the Ferraris finishing 1-2 as Moss suffered an engine failure having put the Vanwall on pole.

Tragically though, Collins died a fortnight later at Nürburgring. He lost control of his Ferrari trying to keep up with Brooks's Vanwall and was thrown out and against a tree, succumbing to head injuries in a Bonn hospital. In just a month, Ferrari had lost two of its works drivers, and Hawthorn two of his teammates and friends.

But it was the events of the Portuguese GP three weeks later that would ultimately decide the championship in a great demonstration of sportsmanship. Moss took pole and fought an early duel with Hawthorn before pulling away. The points system in those days was 8-6-4-3-2 to the first five finishers with an

Left Stirling Moss rounding the Gazometre hairpin at the 1955 Monaco Grand Prix.

Opposite Hawthorn and his Ferrari on the grid before the '57 French GP at Rouen.

Right Hawthorn on the brakes for the Gazometre hairpin at Monaco in '57. He was later involved in a multi-car accident at the chicane, without injury.

additional point for fastest lap and a driver's best six results to count from the 11 races.

In his book *All My Races*, Moss relates: "I was a minute ahead with fastest lap under my belt. Then came the mistake that cost me the World Championship. In the closing stages the Vanwall pits signalled me 'HAW-REC' ('Hawthorn Record') meaning that Mike had set the fastest lap, but I misread it as 'HAW-REG' ('Hawthorn Regular'), which suggested that he was lapping steadily but not particularly quickly." And so, Moss decided not to go for another flier and bring his Vanwall home. Coming into the last laps, Hawthorn, lying second but almost a lap down, spun his Ferrari and stalled the engine. Although he managed to bump-start the car himself downhill, without outside assistance, in their post-race deliberations the stewards threatened to exclude him. To get his Ferrari moving and the engine turning over Hawthorn briefly mounted the pavement of the street circuit going in the opposite direction of the track, an automatic disqualification.

Displaying great sportsmanship, Moss stepped forward and explained that his rival had used an area of pavement which was not designated as the race track and so was not travelling against the direction of the circuit. Hawthorn's second place was restored, as was his point for fastest lap. Some in the pitlane thought he'd been too honourable, as speaking up for Mike had denied Vanwall a 1-2 finish, but Moss was more upset with his pitboard mistake. "Misreading that pit signal really irritated me! I'm sure I could have taken that record back if only I'd realized."

Post-Portugal, Hawthorn led the championship race by four points with two rounds remaining, despite just the single victory

against Moss's three. At the penultimate round in Monza, Moss's gearbox broke after just 17 laps and it was Vanwall teammate Brooks 'going Harry flatters' who was able to add to his victories at Spa and Nürburgring, with Hawthorn following him home.

The Ferrari driver had arrived in Casablanca, Morocco, for the final race in a despondent mood. He had been badly affected by the deaths of Musso and Collins and his mindset was not helped when he discovered that, with the race numbers on the cars not fixed in those days, he had been allocated number 2, the same number used by both Musso and Collins at the time of their deaths. Fortunately, Olivier Gendebien, number 6 on the entry list, agreed to swap.

To win the title Moss needed to win with the fastest lap and have Hawthorn finish third or below. Phil Hill, who had made an impressive Ferrari debut at Monza, was tasked with a hare role in the hope of breaking Moss's Vanwall, but Stirling was at his best that day and won comfortably with that extra point for fastest lap. Stuart Lewis-Evans, who had qualified third on the grid, crashed out when his transmission locked, sending the Vanwall into a fiery accident from which he was extricated barely alive. Teammate Tony Brooks suffered engine failure and so, in the closing stages, Phil Hill was able to move over and allow Hawthorn through into a championship-clinching second place. Despite just the lone win to Moss's four, Hawthorn took the title with 42 points to Moss's 41. That fastest lap point in Portugal, not to mention Moss's sportsmanship, had proven decisive.

But there was no exultation at the flag. As he pulled up in front of the Ferrari garage he was clapped on the back by

well-wishers including the man he had just beaten. "You did it, you old so-and-so," Moss told him. The debonair, bow-tied gentleman racer was surprisingly quiet.

"He was quite strange – he didn't want to know anyone," girlfriend Jean Haworth told Hawthorn biographer Chris Nixon. "He walked me away from the circuit with everyone trying to get him back. He just wanted to get to the hotel for some peace and quiet and he was worried about Stuart Lewis-Evans, for the news of him was not good. And Olivier Gendebien had had a big accident, too."

Gendebien escaped with a couple of broken ribs, but Lewis-Evans was flown back to a specialist burns unit in London where he died six days later.

"Until then," Moss said much later, "winning the championship meant everything to me, but after that it lost meaning. I still wanted to win it, of course, but it didn't matter that much. And looking back, I'm glad in a way that I didn't win it – not just once, anyway. Some pretty average drivers have won it once. I'd rather be remembered as the guy who should have won, and never did …"

Hawthorn didn't live long to enjoy his success. Few were aware that he had a kidney condition that led to blackouts and which was likely to prove fatal, perhaps in the not-too-distant future. Whether that was a factor in his retirement decision at the end of 1958, or whether the loss of Collins "mon ami, mate" had been the determining factor, is not known.

In the late morning of Thursday 22 January 1959, Hawthorn was stood on the forecourt of his Tourist Trophy Garage in Farnham, Surrey – inherited from his father who had died in a road crash

five years previously – when a certain Rob Walker, Moss's entrant remember, slowed on the road outside in his Mercedes 300 SLR and proffered a friendly V-sign.

Hawthorn leapt into his non-standard Jaguar road car and gave chase, waving at Walker as he caught the Mercedes on the Guildford bypass and went by. Shortly afterwards, Walker could only watch as Hawthorn lost it in wet, gusty conditions on a right-hand bend, spun, clipped the back of a truck travelling in the opposite direction and went across the road and into the only tree for a hundred yards. At just 29, Britain's first World Champion was dead.

Moss, as he predicted soon after his retirement, has become famous as the greatest driver who didn't win the World Championship. He eventually patched up his differences with Enzo Ferrari and drove his sportscars. He would have driven F1 cars for the Scuderia in 1962, but for the career-ending injury at Goodwood that almost took his life. There is, perhaps, no finer tribute than by Il Commendatore. In his memoirs Enzo Ferrari placed Moss alongside pre-war ace Tazio Nuvolari as "Men who on any kind of machine, in any circumstances and over any kind of course risked everything to win, and in the ultimate analysis appeared to stand out among the rest. They knew how to get the best whether out of a saloon car, a sports two-seater or a single seat racing car."

Clark vs. Surtees

Clark
25 Grand Prix wins
2 Championships

Surtees
6 Grand Prix wins
1 Championship

There is a perennial debate – usually when one driver is dominating F1 – about who is the greatest of all time, whether it be Fangio, Senna, Prost, Schumacher or Lewis Hamilton. One name that is always added to this list is Jim Clark.

Born 4 March 1936, into a Scottish farming family, the youngest of five children and the only boy, Clark was educated at Loretto School in Musselburgh. The family farm near Duns in Berwickshire provided ample opportunity to get behind the wheel of a vehicle at an early age, and Clark started competing in hillclimbs and local rallies in a Sunbeam-Talbot.

By 1958, he was racing Jaguar D-Types, the sportscar that had taken Jaguar to victory at Le Mans for three successive years, for the Border Reivers team based in nearby Chirnside and tearing up the track in British club racing. His family were strongly against a professional racing career, but Clark's immense talent behind the wheel was obvious.

That Boxing Day, he raced the Reivers' small Lotus Elite against a certain Colin Chapman, the Lotus founder and a competent driver himself, who took note of Clark's ability behind the wheel of one of his customer cars. In 1959 the Border Reivers entered the Elite in Le Mans and Clark finished 10th before Chapman asked him to drive in the newly introduced Formula Junior category the following year.

Joining Clark in that first race was John Surtees who was already a celebrity, a motorsport World Champion on two wheels. Born 11 February 1934 – a couple of years older than Clark – he was the son of Jack Surtees, a South London motorcycle dealer and part-time grasstrack racer. Surtees Junior started racing at grasstrack meetings from the age of 15 and joined the Vincent motorcycle company as an apprentice. He also got the chance to race on tarmac and first came to prominence when, as a 17-year-old, he challenged Norton ace Geoff Duke in two races at Thruxton in 1951 – Duke would be World Champion at 350cc and 500cc that same year.

Surtees was taken on as a works rider by Norton in 1955 and shone, before the company hit financial problems which propelled him towards the Italian MV Agusta factory team headed by the aristocratic Count Domenici Agusta.

In 1956 Surtees won the 500cc World Championship for Agusta, his first title and their first title, a feat he repeated in 1958, 1959 and 1960, accompanied by three World Championships at 350cc. He eclipsed Geoff Duke's records and became the first man to win the Isle of Man Senior TT three years in a row.

A switch to grand prix racing had first been suggested to him in 1958 when he sat alongside Mike Hawthorn, the new Formula 1 World Champion, at the BBC's Sport Personality of the Year award ceremony. Like the F1 series of the 1950s, there were between six and eight races making up the motorcycle World Championship, and with his boss Count Agusta unenthusiastic about Surtees riding other machinery, it left a lot of time on his hands. In late 1959 (having won the BBC Sports Personality of the Year that year), he was offered the chance to drive an Aston Martin DBR1 sportscar at Goodwood, lapping the car quicker than it had ever gone before. Team boss Reg Parnell was not slow to offer him a deal but Surtees turned it down to do one more year of bike racing.

On hearing about the Aston Martin test, boss of the Vanwall F1 team Tony Vandervell was quickly on the phone offering Surtees the opportunity to find out what he could do in his F1 car. Also testing at Goodwood, Surtees lapped the Sussex track, matching and then beating times previously set by Stirling Moss in the same car.

While Surtees' motorcycle contract was explicit as far as two-wheel racing was concerned, Count Agusta had failed to make any provision against his rider trying the occasional four-wheel race, providing it didn't clash with a championship round. To introduce himself to this new challenge, Surtees decided to buy himself one of the new Formula Junior cars, a Cooper T52 and compete in the races that his 1960 schedule allowed. However, before he could get his chequebook out, future F1 team owner Ken Tyrrell signed him to his fledgling team. He would be entered in a Formula Junior race at Goodwood; his first race against Jimmy Clark, and more significantly, his first ever race on four wheels.

Amazingly, on his racing debut, he put the car on pole position and was leading the race and the works Lotus Junior of Clark until his lack of racecraft allowed him to be tripped up by a backmarker, allowing Clark through for the win.

Running cars in various formulae Colin Chapman's introduction of the rear-engined Lotus 18 in 1960 had transformed his Formula 1 team's prospects. He had the swaggering, hell-raising figure of Innes Ireland as one of his contracted drivers and decided to test him against Surtees at Silverstone. Once again, Surtees proved fastest, and Chapman wasted no time in promoting John to the Grand Prix team. Incredibly, just 10 weeks after his first race on four wheels he was lining up for one of the greatest tests of a racing driver's

precision and nerve, the Monaco Grand Prix. He qualified 15th of the 24 starters but a transmission failure after 17 laps meant his first race ended in a DNF. The better news for Chapman was that Stirling Moss's privately entered Lotus 18 won the race.

The schedule of motorcycle races didn't allow Surtees back into the F1 paddock until July, when he finished a magnificent second behind Jack Brabham at the British Grand Prix at Silverstone, in what was only his second F1 race. For his third race, the Portuguese Grand Prix, he stuck the Lotus on pole, half a second clear of Moss in a similar Lotus. Surtees led until a petrol leak coated his pedals, his foot slipped off the brake and he crashed, irreparably damaging his radiator.

Clark, meanwhile, made his Formula 1 debut for Team Lotus at the Dutch Grand Prix of 1960 (one that Surtees couldn't attend) qualifying 11th with teammate Innes Ireland substantially further up the grid in third. His race was cut short by transmission failure, a familiar Lotus flaw.

That season Clark would contest six races for Lotus in F1 compared to Surtees' four. The acid test of any F1 driver rivalry is their results while driving the same machinery, and in the two races they competed against each other in 1960 honours were shared. In Portugal Surtees took pole to Clark's 8th, and in the final grand prix of the season, the USGP at Riverside, Clark finished fifth in qualifying with Surtees a tenth of a second behind in sixth place and the third Team Lotus driver, Innes Ireland, a substantial 1.2 seconds further back, but still in seventh place.

In the race, Surtees ran ahead of Clark, but spun in front of him and was hit by the Scotsman, sending Surtees into retirement and

Right After falling out with Ferrari in '66, Surtees joined Cooper and qualified second to Lorenzo Bandini's Modena machine in the French GP at Reims. Both retired.

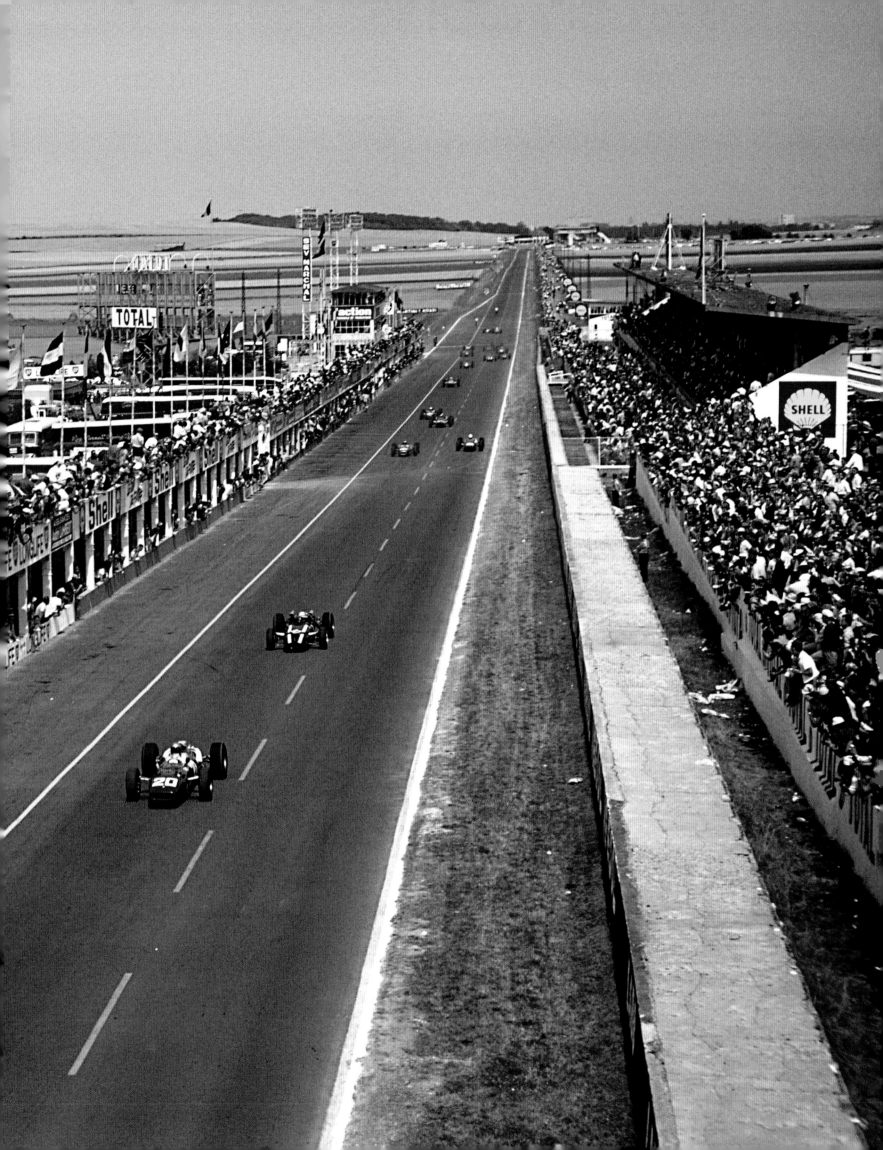

Above Clark with Jackie Stewart at the '66 Italian GP.

Opposite Clark and his Lotus-Climax in classic pose en route to pole position at Monaco in '66.

Clark for pit stop repairs. Despite retirements in three out of four races, team boss Colin Chapman had seen enough to determine who would be his No.1 driver for 1961. He offered Surtees team leader status for the following season and the opportunity to pick his teammate in what would now be a two-car team. Surtees opted to drive with Clark.

On finding out that he was no longer required, the blustering Innes Ireland, who had a contract for 1961, demanded to know what Chapman thought he was doing letting this upstart from bikes call the shots. Ireland's outrage at being passed over played large in the motorsport press and Surtees became so worn down by the dispute that he decided to walk away. Enzo Ferrari was also keen to sign the Englishman, but Surtees was wary of signing for the Scuderia. Having raced for MV Agusta he knew the pressure the Italian media could bring to bear if things didn't go well and after all, he was still just a rookie with four races to his name.

The 1961 season was not to be the breakthrough year for either driver, with Surtees signing for Reg Parnell's F1 team running a Cooper T53-Climax and finishing the season 11th in the Word Championship, his best finishes two fifth places at Spa and the Nürburgring. Clark managed to get on the podium for the Dutch and French Grands Prix, but was involved in a terrible accident at Monza with the World-Champion-in-waiting, Wolfgang von Trips.

The aristocratic German driver in the 'sharknose' Ferrari 156 was leading the championship and on pole for the penultimate race of the season, the Italian Grand Prix. However, when the flag dropped, he got a terrible start and was enveloped by the leading bunch, slipping back down the order behind Clark who had

started from seventh on the grid. Von Trips overtook him into Vialone (now Ascari) but failed to appreciate that Clark was slipstreaming him down the following straight towards Parabolica (now Albereto). When the Scot moved out for an overtaking move, Von Trips turned in not realizing he was there. He clipped the Lotus's front wheel which sent the Ferrari up a bank and along a fence lined with spectators, killing 14 of them. The driver was flung dead onto the track. Clark stopped, in deep shock at what had just happened. However, this being Formula 1 of the 1960s, the race continued …

Success was to come for Team Lotus in 1962. Colin Chapman's revolutionary Lotus 25, built with a monocoque chassis, was a technical innovation that every team would eventually copy. Clark won the Belgian, British and US Grands Prix and also took six pole positions. Jimmy should have won his first title, but in the season-closing South African Grand Prix in East London, an oil leak 20 laps from the end while leading, sent him into retirement and allowed BRM's Graham Hill to become champion, in much the same way that Phil Hill had inherited the title destined for Von Trips the previous year. Surtees managed two podiums in his Lola Mk4 and finished the season a respectable fourth, despite only five finishes.

Clark made up for his disappointment in 1963, taking seven pole positions in a fully sorted Lotus 25 and seven victories from the season's 10 races on the way to becoming World Champion. One of his best performances came at Spa, a place that taxed a driver's qualities but also allowed a virtuoso to display them. Clark's exceptional performances there were achieved in the face of an intense dislike of a circuit he viewed as dangerous.

In his first Belgian GP in 1960, Clark's Lotus teammate Alan Stacey was killed. Still in the days of open-face helmets, Stacey was hit in the face by a bird and crashed just after the Burnenville corner. Clark associated Spa with tragedy from that point on, but it did not stop him driving and winning there in four consecutive years, starting in 1962. His 1963 drive in torrential rain stands out, beating second-place man Bruce McLaren by almost five minutes. However, he was not immune to danger. He refused to race at Le Mans after 1961, with its inclusion of amateur drivers and machinery of vastly different performance.

Clark and Chapman also shook up the Indianapolis establishment when they finished second behind Parnelli Jones in a first visit to the Indy 500 in 1963. It probably should have been first as Jones's Offenhauser-powered car sprayed oil all over the track and Clark backed off, certain that Jones would be black-flagged. Had it been an American car behind, he probably would have been. Ever sporting, Clark called it "a damn fine drive" from Jones and contented himself with almost half the runners-up prize of $55,000, more than any 'foreigner' had ever taken away from Indianapolis.

Ford funded Chapman's entry in a bid to win the 500 and the money was an undoubted attraction. The $125,000 prize money on offer was more than Team Lotus could earn in a complete year of Formula 1. They were back in 1964, but hampered by Dunlop tyres that threw a tread and destroyed the rear suspension.

Despite concerns from his mother, who had noted the fiery accidents the race could produce, Clark returned to Indy in 1965 and this time he won it, claiming the first victory by a non-American for 49 years and the first for a British driver and British car.

He was delighted with the £46,000 he took home, an awful lot of money in 1965, when his F1 earnings for winning his second World Championship and six races, amounted to around £13,500. It also put him on the radar of the inland revenue, sending him into tax exile in Bermuda.

Surtees had spent the 1963 season driving for Ferrari and finished in fourth place again, but it was a year that gave him his debut grand prix victory at the Nürburgring. With Ferrari in the ascendancy, the 1964 season looked like it might come down to a battle between Clark and Surtees. The two were still good friends, far from the intense dislike and enmity fostered by some rival drivers in the 1970s and 1980s. "He actually introduced me to my first wife," Surtees recalled to *Autosport* on the 40th anniversary of Clark's death. "I was woken up by a lot of noise in the hotel at the Belgian Grand Prix and it was Jimmy and this girl dancing. He was actually my best man at our wedding."

The 1964 season went down to the wire after Surtees had won both Nürburgring and Monza from pole. Clark could boast wins at Zandvoort, Spa and Brands Hatch but it was Graham Hill driving a BRM who led going to the final round in Mexico. He had 39 points to the 34 of Surtees and Clark's 30. With only the six best results to count, however, Hill could only improve his score by finishing higher than fourth. Clark would be champion if he won with Surtees not higher than third and Hill not higher than fourth.

Clark led away from pole and looked comfortable, with Dan Gurney running second and Hill and Surtees' Ferrari teammate Lorenzo Bandini disputing third, while Surtees initially ran fifth. Bandini then hit the back of Hill and damaged an exhaust pipe,

causing the BRM to lose power. It was looking good for Clark. If it stayed the same, he and Hill would both have 39 points and Jim would win four to two on a win countback.

Then, disaster. An oil line failed on the Lotus and the engine seized just as Clark started the last lap … Hill's strangled engine had by now allowed Surtees through into third, the order now Gurney-Bandini-Surtees. Frantic waving from the Ferrari pit alerted Bandini to the fact that his team leader was now behind him and could win the championship if he pulled over, which the Italian duly did. Surtees beat Hill to the title by a single point. But with a little bit of extra mechanical luck, Clark could so easily have been a World Champion in 1962 and 1964, however 1965 brought him his second title behind the wheel of the all-conquering Lotus 33. He won the first six grands prix of a nine-race season, Surtees in a Ferrari 158 was well off the pace.

The two friends were drifting apart. "When you joined a team like Ferrari in those days," Surtees told *Autosport,* "you isolated yourself quite a lot from the British contingent, so my relationship with Jim didn't develop after those early years, but we remained friends."

In terms of finding competitive cockpits, Jimmy's luck was better than John's. A principled and determined character who liked to do things his own way, Surtees fell victim to Ferrari politics in 1966. He had a prickly relationship with Ferrari's racing director Eugenio Dragoni and when Ferrari had to cut its Le Mans 1966 entry from three cars to two, Surtees told Dragoni that as he was quicker than Ludovico Scarfiotti, he should start the race, run flat-out and try to break what was likely to be a stern Ford GT40 challenge.

Dragoni, however, had other ideas. Scarfiotti was the nephew of Fiat boss Gianni Agnelli, who was going to be present, and so it would be nice if Ludovico could start the race. If that was one in the eye for 'Il Grande John' then too bad, Dragoni would pair Scarfiotti with Mike Spence instead and, with Bandini and Frenchman Jean Guichet in the other car, Surtees would not be required.

Officially, Dragoni said that he was not sure that Surtees was properly recovered from a life-threatening crash in a Lola T70 sportscar at Mosport in Canada the previous September. Which was a little odd given that Surtees had just brilliantly won the Belgian GP at Spa by 42 seconds the previous weekend …

Surtees was incensed and, when there was no support from Enzo Ferrari, he severed his links with the team immediately, mid-season. In F1, he went off to drive a Cooper-Maserati alongside the emerging Jochen Rindt, who had won Le Mans in 1965 and was regarded as potentially one of the quickest men on the F1 grid. Rindt was only in his second season and would go on to become World Champion four years later, but Surtees proved his undoubted pace by outqualifying the Austrian six to one over the remainder of the season and winning the final race in Mexico.

Clark continued with Lotus in 1966, but both men had to cede to Jack Brabham's team as 'Black Jack' took the world title in 1966 and teammate Denny Hulme in 1967. Surtees had switched to the new Honda team that year and to the Japanese team's delight, gave them a first grand prix win at Monza, a power circuit. Things were looking up for Jimmy too, with the introduction of the Lotus 49. Fully sorted by the end of the 1967 season, Clark took the final two races at Watkins Glen and Mexico City. When he won the first race

of 1968, the South African GP, from pole it looked odds on that this would be the year of his third world title.

The motor racing world was left stunned when news came through that he had died in an inconsequential Formula 2 race at a cold, drizzly Hockenheim in early April 1968. A suspected rear puncture sent his Lotus off into the trees and killed him instantly. Amid a particularly perilous era, a common thought from drivers in the pitlane was, 'If it can happen to Jim Clark, what chance have we got?' Clark was renowned for being 'light' on his cars – given four Lotus gearboxes his mechanic could tell which was Clark's by the lack of wear.

Surtees drove on until 1972 in increasingly uncompetitive machinery, but never again reached the kind of results he achieved when pitted against Clark. In 2008 he paid tribute to his friend and the career-long relationship he had with Lotus boss Colin Chapman. "They made a very strong combination and you didn't enjoy them as opponents, although you had to appreciate that it was something rather special. When something like that comes to an end in that fashion like that, it's very sad."

At the time, Juan Manuel Fangio labelled the Scot, "outstandingly the greatest grand prix driver of all time," and there is no finer tribute. Clark's greatness is beyond doubt. But although the numbers tell you that he won 25 grands prix and Surtees just six, such a statistic badly undermines Big John's level, just as six wins sells Gilles Villeneuve drastically short. It's all about getting into the right cockpits and Surtees simply did not do that often enough. Many still lament the fact that in 1961 it could have been Clark and Surtees competing together for Team Lotus.

Stewart vs. Rindt

Stewart
27 Grand Prix wins
3 Championships

Rindt
6 Grand Prix wins
1 Championship

The early 1960s in Formula 1 was very much the Jim Clark era, the soft-spoken Scottish border farmer winning the first of his two World Championships in 1963. But there was another great Scot, John Young 'Jackie' Stewart, who would follow in his wheel-tracks and eventually surpass Clark's then-record 25 GP victories.

Stewart was born in Dumbarton on 11 June 1939, to parents who ran the local Dumbuck Garage. He was eight years younger than brother Jimmy, himself a talented sportscar driver in the 1950s for the famous Ecurie Ecosse team and then as a works driver for both Jaguar and Aston Martin. It was watching Jimmy at hillclimbs and ever more prestigious races, culminating in the 1953 British Grand Prix at Silverstone, that gave 'wee Jackie' the racing bug.

But there was a problem. The Stewarts' mother, Jeanie, despite being a huge motoring enthusiast, got so anxious about Jimmy's involvement in what was then so often a lethal sport, that she came out in a rash and would seek medical treatment. That, on top of accidents at Le Mans and Nürburgring, persuaded Jimmy Stewart to retire from racing at just 24.

So, when a wealthy customer (Dumbuck Garage was a Jaguar dealer) started to offer an 18-year-old Jackie races in his own cars, it was done very much on the quiet, Stewart competing under the moniker 'A.N. Other'. Local curiosity was piqued when A.N. Other started winning all the time … Still, the secret did not emerge until Stewart married Helen McGregor from nearby Helensburgh in 1962.

Jackie was also a talented clay pigeon shot, narrowly missing out on a place in the 1960 Rome Olympic team, but the caption under a picture of their wedding referred to 'the talented racing driver', not the talented shooter. The cat was out of the bag.

It was still a tough call for Jackie to further his racing ambitions professionally, against his mother's wishes.

Meanwhile, Jochen Rindt, three years Stewart's junior, had been born on 18 August 1942, to German Karl Rindt and Ilse Martinowitz, from Graz in Austria. The family spice mill, Klein & Rindt, was based in Mainz on the river Rhine, where Jochen was born, but also had a branch in Hamburg, which is where Jochen's parents were killed in the July 1943 Operation Gomorrah RAF/USAAF firebombing designed to crush German morale and end the Second World War. Jochen himself had been evacuated to Austria. Subsequently brought up by his maternal grandparents, he would race with an Austrian licence and regarded that as his nationality, never German.

A talented skier and tennis player, Rindt did everything on the limit and after learning to drive on family land, was tearing up Austrian roads long before he ought to have been, along with fellow-Austrian soulmate and now Red Bull Racing consultant, Helmut Marko. The pair attended their first grand prix together at the Nürburgring in 1961, where they threw their support behind Ferrari driver Wolfgang von Trips, then in contention to become World Champion.

A couple of months later, in a prelude to Jochen's own fate, Von Trips collided with Clark on the approach to Monza's Parabolica (now Alboreto). The tragedy did not deter Rindt who raced in Austria and Italy with a Simca, then Alfa Romeo saloon, fully supported by grandparents. When he inherited Klein & Rindt on his 21st birthday he promptly bought, first, a Formula Junior Cooper to race in Europe in 1963, then a Brabham Formula 2 car for 1964.

Trying to make his own way as a driver back then was a certain Frank Williams who, after himself crashing at the Nürburgring, spent the rest of the race watching Rindt, who he thought was just magic. And, later, it was being overtaken by Jochen at some unimaginable speed and angle, in an F2 race that persuaded future president of the Fédération Internationale de l'Automobile (FIA) Max Mosley that he should abandon his own racing ambitions.

It was in 1964 that Stewart and Rindt both made their mark, Jochen in Formula 2 and Jackie in Formula 3. Goodwood circuit manager Robin Mackay had been watching when Stewart set a new sportscar lap record at the Sussex track and spoke of his potential to a friend, Ken Tyrrell, who was in the process of setting up a team for the first year of a new Formula 3 and on the lookout for a new young driver.

Stewart's ambition back then was to make a living driving touring and GT cars for teams like Ecurie Ecosse and he wasn't so sure about single-seaters. He phoned Jim Clark for advice and Jim told him that if he wanted to be a top driver he had to drive single-seaters one day. And, if he was going to do that, then Ken Tyrrell was the guy to drive for.

Tyrrell would run the works Cooper Formula 3 cars and John Cooper was there on the day in March when Stewart had his first run in the new car. So, too, was Bruce McLaren, then a two-time grand prix winner and a works Cooper F1 driver for the past five years. McLaren and Stewart took turns driving the car and it was Jackie who ended up with the day's fastest lap.

"You've got to sign him!" John Cooper told Tyrrell. So, that night, instead of driving back to Scotland, Jackie found himself at Tyrrell's house for dinner. Ken offered him £10,000 up front, a colossal amount of money back then. At the time, Jackie and Helen Stewart had £50 in the bank. But JYS, as he would become known in the racing world, always championed the importance of mind management, so he calmed himself down, resisted the temptation to shake on the deal there and then, and quietly asked if there was an alternative.

Yes, said Tyrrell, £5 up front and then 50% of all the prize and bonus money you earn with the team. After thinking it over, Jackie demonstrated the faith he had in his own ability by taking the £5 deal. Given that over an 11-year period he would lose 57 friends and colleagues to racing accidents, it was also a brave move.

Rindt, meanwhile, had arrived in the UK, now seen as the centre of the motor-racing world. With some backing from Ford Austria he took a Brabham to the Mallory Park circuit in Leicestershire for Whit Sunday's Grovewoood Trophy F2 race. Never having seen the place before, he put the Brabham on pole after asking Denny Hulme if he could follow him around for a few laps.

"I was very surprised," Jochen admitted. But probably not as surprised as the likes of Jim Clark and Hulme. In the race, Rindt messed up his start but turned in a strong recovery drive to finish third. Then he hitched the Brabham onto a trailer, drove to Crystal Palace and the next day beat a field including Clark and Graham Hill, to win the London Trophy. He had truly arrived. Before that weekend, Rindt's BP sponsorship was worth £25 a race. It was immediately upped to £1,200 for the season but more significantly, BP's competition boss was instrumental in persuading John Cooper to offer Rindt an F1 drive for 1965.

Opposite Left to right: John Surtees, Denny Hulme, Bob Bondurant, Jochen Rindt, Jackie Stewart, Graham Hill, Lorenzo Bandini, Innes Ireland at the 1966 Mexican Grand Prix in Mexico City.

Left Rindt and his Brabham in the pits ahead of the wet, foggy '68 German GP at Nürburgring.

Below Rindt's Brabham, Stewart's Matra and Jackie Ickx's Ferrari share the front row for the '68 French GP at Rouen.

Above Stewart in the '68 Canadian GP at Mont-Tremblant.

Right The Ferraris of pole position man Jacky Ickx and Chris Amon at the start of the '68 German GP. Amid appalling conditions, Stewart make great use of demon Dunlop rain tyres to win by more than four minutes in what many regard as his best ever drive.

Opposite After taking pole, Rindt's Brabham retired from the '68 French GP with a fuel leak.

At the same time, Stewart was going great guns in F3, cleaning up the British championship and winning the prestigious Monaco race as well as the support race to the French Grand Prix at Rouen, something which brought him an F1 offer from BRM for 1965. By the end of the season he also had offers from Cooper and Lotus. Using his calm, logical analysis, Stewart decided that Cooper had lost its way in F1 since winning back-to-back world titles in 1959–60, that Lotus was the domain of friend and undisputed No.1 Clark, and so opted for BRM.

And so it was that Stewart and Rindt, the new F1 young talents with BRM and Cooper respectively, found themselves in the same King's Arms Hotel in the South African coastal city of East London, nervously awaiting their World Championship debuts in the South African GP on New Year's day 1965. Deciding it best not to get involved in New Year's Eve revelry breaking out at the hotel, they went to watch a local drive-in movie together. And would remain firm friends as well as rivals.

Stewart finished third in the championship in his first F1 season, behind Clark and Graham Hill, and took his first F1 victory at Monza. Rindt had a more difficult time as he and teammate Bruce McLaren struggled with the less competitive Cooper. There was a bit of a reversal in 1966 as Stewart and BRM fought against unreliability, Jackie dropping to seventh in the championship despite taking the first of his three Monaco Grand Prix victories. Rindt, meanwhile, rose to third behind Jack Brabham and John Surtees.

The race at Spa in 1966 was pivotal for a couple of key reasons. The whole field, on slick tyres, was suddenly confronted by a soaking road on the daunting Spa-Francorchamps, then an 8-mile blindingly quick lap with no barriers and exposed hedges, walls, telegraph poles and even houses.

Jack Brabham got a huge fright when he missed hitting a house by a hair's breadth, a complete passenger as his car aquaplaned. Without quite the same stomach for the race afterwards, he was nevertheless deeply impressed by the manner in which Rindt went by him on the wet road and led until overhauled by Surtees' Ferrari as the road dried.

Stewart, meanwhile, had aquaplaned off the circuit, destroyed a woodcutter's hut, glanced a telegraph pole and then disappeared down a bank, coming to rest on a farmhouse patio, trapped in a BRM chassis now bent out of shape, with leaking fuel around him. It was an inferno waiting to happen. BRM teammate Graham Hill and American Bob Bondurant stopped and borrowed a tool kit from a spectator, removed the steering wheel from Jackie's car and hauled him out. When Stewart was finally loaded into an ambulance with back and rib injuries, it got lost en route to hospital. It was this incident that prompted JYS to become such a determined safety campaigner in the sport, often in the face of hostility from organizers, journalists and even fellow drivers.

Rindt's already flat, boxer's nose was then put further out of joint when John Surtees fell out with Ferrari team manager Eugenio Dragoni, left the team and joined Cooper, scuppering what was then Jochen's No.1 status with the team. It's fair to say that 'Big John' got the upper hand before leaving for Honda at the end of the season.

Left Jackie Stewart leads Jacky Ickx in the 1971 Spanish GP at Montjuïc Park, Barcelona.

Neither Stewart nor Rindt enjoyed 1967, both finishing just two races. Stewart dropped to ninth in the championship with podiums in Belgium and France as BRM fought unreliability with its complex H16 engine. And all Rindt had to show for his season were a couple of fourth places with the unwieldy Maserati V12-powered Cooper.

Both sought different teams for 1968, Stewart renewing his partnership with Tyrrell as Ken ran a Cosworth-powered French Matra chassis, and Rindt joining Brabham, champions of the previous two seasons, as reigning Drivers' Champion Denny Hulme left to start his partnership with Bruce McLaren who, like Jack Brabham, was now constructing his own cars for his nascent McLaren team.

Stewart went right down to the wire for the championship in Mexico, losing out at the final round to Graham Hill's Lotus after Lotus team leader Clark had perished in a Formula 2 accident at Hockenheim. Rindt, however, despite high hopes at Brabham, suffered more engine unreliability, this time with Brabham's new Repco motors.

Although Jochen Rindt had car control second to none and drove in a spectacular tail-out manner, he, like Stewart, was keenly aware of the dangers of his profession. Brabhams were renowned for their solid construction and strength, while Lotuses were fast but fragile. After Clark's death, Stewart and Rindt were perhaps the quickest drivers on the grid, although some thought the aggressive style that saw Jochen an undisputed king of F2, was holding him back in F1 with heavier cars and more complex tyre wear. The renowned journalist Denis Jenkinson professed that Rindt would never win a grand prix and even offered to shave off his distinguishing beard if it ever happened. Lotus boss Colin Chapman had faith in Jochen though, and offered him a Lotus seat for 1969.

Rindt discussed the wisdom of it with friend and manager Bernie Ecclestone, who remembered, "We had the choice for Jochen of the Goodyear deal with Brabham or the Firestone deal with Lotus. I said to him, 'If you want to win the World Championship you've got more chance with Lotus than with Brabham. If you want to stay alive, you've got more chance with Brabham than with Lotus.' It wasn't a bad thing to say: it was a matter of fact."

Rindt, in 1969, drove the same Cosworth-powered Lotus 49 that had taken Graham Hill to the previous year's title and he had no doubt that he was quicker than his new teammate. Stewart, meanwhile, would have Matra's new MS80 for his title campaign. By now, Jackie and Jochen and their respective wives, Helen and Nina, were as close as you could really be in such a competitive environment, along with Piers and Sally Courage.

Stewart started the 1969 season with wins in South Africa and then Spain, where Rindt had led before the new high-mounted rear aerofoil on his Lotus snapped and sent him into the barrier, collecting the wreckage of teammate Hill's Lotus, which had suffered a similar failure. He suffered cuts and a broken nose, missing Monaco. Successive wins in Holland and France gave Stewart a healthy championship lead as they came to the British Grand Prix at Silverstone.

It was one of the greatest Formula 1 races of all time as Stewart and Rindt exchanged the lead more than 30 times. With the Lotus a

Opposite Rindt's Lotus 49 leads the '69 Spanish GP in Barcelona before his tall rear aerofoil broke and sent him into the wreckage of teammate Graham Hill's sister car, which had suffered an identical failure.

Left By round three in Monaco a fortnight later, the ever-growing wings had been banned. This is Stewart's Matra running without them in Monte Carlo.

Below The Lotus 49s of pole man Rindt and Graham Hill sandwich Stewart's Lotus on the grid for the Dutch GP in '69.

Above Rindt aboard the beautiful Lotus 72, in which he would win four successive 1970 GPs before crashing fatally in practice for the Italian GP at Monza, becoming the sport's only posthumous World Champion.

Right Rindt was something of a trendsetter, sometimes wearing a full-length fur coat when it was cold, sometimes paired with Aviator shades. "On most people it would have looked ridiculous, but on him it looked magnificent", said a young and impressionable Niki Lauda.

Opposite Rindt and close friend Stewart, whose nod to fashion was the dark shades paired with a black corduroy cap.

tad quicker than the Matra on the straight, Jochen tended to pass on the Hangar Straight into Stowe, while Jackie would re-pass into Woodcote as the pair contested their own race. Bruce McLaren, lapped by them, observed: "While most believed Jochen was on the ragged edge while Jackie drove coolly and calmly, when they both lapped me, the reverse applied."

Stewart regards the battle as the most pleasurable of his career. Although Rindt looked like he had the edge in the closing stages, the Lotus rear wing endplate failed and started to foul his tyre, Jackie pointing back towards it as he went by. Then, adding insult to injury, Rindt ran short of fuel and required a late pit stop, relegating him to fourth. "Jackie isn't just winning his races this year, he's winning mine as well!" Jochen said later.

Stewart clinched his first World Championship in another fantastic race at Monza. A typical slipstreamer, a blanket would have covered Stewart, Rindt, McLaren and Jackie's Matra teammate Jean-Pierre Beltoise as they started the last lap. Into Parabolica (now Alboreto for the last time, Beltoise came down the inside, braked too late and went in too deep. Stewart crossed the line no more than a foot in front of Rindt as 0.19 seconds covered the top four. Cannily, Stewart and Ken Tyrrell had gone for a high third gear and a very long fourth to avoid losing fractions making the change to fifth gear in the sprint to the line. Two races later, Jochen finally claimed victory in the season's richest race, the $50,000 US Grand Prix at Watkins Glen. And to the delight of many in the pitlane off came the sanctimonious Denis Jenkinson's beard.

Stewart's title defence was hampered in 1970 by Matra wanting to run a V12 engine and Tyrrell electing instead to switch to the new March chassis which, despite Stewart winning in Spain, was not fully competitive and certainly not a match for Colin Chapman's groundbreaking Lotus 72.

Rindt, who some accused of arrogance, never had the easiest of relationships with Chapman, but finally it all seemed to be coming good. In another classic F1 race, Rindt forced Jack Brabham into a mistake at the final corner on the last lap to score a fantastic Monaco victory in the old Lotus 49. Rindt then scored four successive wins in the new 72 at Zandvoort, Clermont-Ferrand, Brands Hatch and Hockenheim. After breaking down at his home race at the Österreichring, Jochen went to Monza in early September on the verge of his life's ambition.

It had been an awful year. Both drivers had lost close friends. Bruce McLaren had died testing a McLaren CanAm car at Goodwood in early June and Piers Courage lost his life in the Dutch Grand Prix not three weeks later. And now, running without a rear wing on his Lotus 72 in practice, Rindt's car snapped left, right, then sharply left under braking for Parabolica, with Hulme's McLaren following. A snapped inboard brake shaft was the suspected cause. The Lotus 72's nose went under the guard rail and the car was wrenched violently around one of the support stanchions, ripping open the front. Seatbelts had been compulsory since 1968, but Jochen hated wearing crutch straps and submarined down the cockpit with the seatbelt buckle inflicting grave injuries to his chest and neck. In the pits, there was unease as Hulme stopped at the Lotus pit, not McLaren.

Stewart, about to go out, heard that something had happened and that it was Jochen. "I sprinted through the crowds

Opposite The Monza pit lane goes quiet as news is awaited following Rindt's crash at Parabolica. McLaren drivers Denny Hulme, following Jochen when it happened, and Peter Gethin (right), can be seen stood by their cars.

Right Rindt celebrates his last-lap win in the 1970 British GP at Brands Hatch with wife Nina.

and arrived at the medical compound, which was fenced in," he recalled in his autobiography. "There was a guard on the gate, who recognized me and let me in. I looked around … and saw Jochen. He was lying on the back of an open Volkswagen pick-up truck and there was nobody attending to him, which shocked me. His head was propped up but his eyes were closed. I saw that he had a serious open wound at his left ankle and foot. It wasn't bleeding. In that moment, I knew Jochen had gone.

"Later, as I prepared to drive, my head was full of sadness, confusion and thoughts of Jochen and Nina. It was too much and I started to cry. I don't think anyone saw because my tinted visor was down. As I accelerated out of the pitlane I could taste the salt of my own tears."

Stewart's third lap was his fastest at Monza. "As I brought the car to a halt, the awful reality of the day overwhelmed me again. The tears started all over again. A friend passed me a bottle of Coca-Cola, I took two swigs and almost unconsciously hurled the bottle with all my force against a concrete wall. It smashed into smithereens. Nobody said a word. That was completely out of character for me, and it never happened again."

Jochen's 45 points remained unsurpassed, Emerson Fittipaldi's win in the US Grand Prix for Lotus ensuring that Ferrari's Jacky Ickx could not overhaul Jochen, who became the sport's only posthumous World Champion.

Jackie – who, along with New Zealander Chris Amon, were the only drivers Rindt regarded as true rivals – was the man who presented Nina Rindt with the World Championship trophy at the FIA awards dinner in Paris.

Stewart regained his championship crown in 1971 and took a third title two years later before announcing his retirement. By then JYS had beaten his friend Jim Clark's record with 27 wins from 99 grands prix. He had raced against the best drivers of the 1960s and early 1970s but told *Motor Sport* magazine: "Across my career it was Jochen Rindt who was the toughest, the most competitive. He was very fast, a very clean racing driver. In 1969 we had some great battles, notably at Silverstone passing and re-passing each other for the lead all the way. Out of Becketts, in the slipstream, we would point to which side we wanted the other to pass." It was another era.

Hunt vs. Lauda

Hunt
10 Grand Prix wins
1 Championship

Lauda
25 Grand Prix wins
3 Championships

The rivalry between Niki Lauda and James Hunt and their epic battle for the 1976 World Championship took motor racing from the back pages of newspapers to the front. It was immortalized in the 2013 movie *Rush* with actors Daniel Brühl and Chris Hemsworth playing Lauda and Hunt respectively.

For suspense and drama, it has arguably never been surpassed in Formula 1's history, although some might argue that the 2021 title fight between Max Verstappen and Lewis Hamilton was even more compelling. But that did not have such a rich vein of sub-plots and side stories and ended with an FIA fiasco.

James Simon Wallis Hunt was born on 29 August 1947, to a Surrey stockbroker, some two and a half years before Andreas Nikolaus Lauda came into the world, to a wealthy Viennese paper manufacturing family.

Hunt, one of six children, was described by his mother as persistently rebellious and prone to temper tantrums, restless, highly active, with great determination to get his own way. Unlike today's F1 stars who are put into karts as soon as they're 'Bambinos' (6–8 years old), it was not until the day before James's 18th birthday that his tennis doubles partner, whose brother was a Mini club racer, suggested they go to a meeting at Silverstone. It was the first time that Hunt realized motor racing was accessible to mere mortals rather than just "foreigners with unpronounceable names".

James, an old Wellingtonian, was supposed to be headed to medical school but, according to biographer Gerald Donaldson, told his parents that same evening, "All your anxieties about my fecklessness are over. I am going to be a racing driver. And I shall be World Champion."

His mother was mortified that instead of saving lives, her son was going to risk his own in an endeavour she saw as unproductive for society. Hunt, meanwhile, had worked out that it would cost his family around £5,000 to put him through medical school, so proposed to his father that, instead, how about £2,500 up front now, to buy his first race car? Predictably rebuffed, Hunt spent the next couple of years taking odd jobs while he painstakingly built a racing Mini with next to no mechanical knowledge.

Over in Austria, Lauda had a more indulgent grandmother and a Mini became a Porsche as Niki contested hillclimbs and local races before turning his attention to Formula Vee single-seaters. Formula 3 racing, both in Britain and Europe, was where it was at for aspiring young stars, but the racing was fraught, accidents common and progress difficult.

By way of example, Hunt's Lotus Formula 3 deal provided the car, expenses for engines/crash repairs and £1,000 towards running costs and travel. Any shortfall needed to be made up from start/ prize money, which at year-end, amounted to a debt of £4,500 for James. Often broke, the less well-heeled would-be aces lived in tents and ate cheaply. At Pau, Hunt crashed in qualifying, couldn't race and didn't get his start money. When someone siphoned fuel from his tow car during the night, James had no money and no means of getting home. He was forced to procure petrol by the same means, creeping around the paddock in the dark trying to find a French car without a locking petrol cap …

Hunt lived on adrenaline, suffered hugely from nerves and was physically sick before every race. He claimed it was fear for his future on the financial and job security side and nothing to do with

the danger, although that would become a factor later on. He was also hot-tempered. When he failed to produce a document with his blood group having driven to Italy for a round at Vallelunga, organizers told him he couldn't race. So, James drove out of the paddock and parked his car at 90 degrees to the front row of the grid so that nobody else could either. It didn't go down well.

Early on, James's behaviour was more notorious than his driving. In a televized Formula 3 race at Crystal Palace he collided with a rival, Dave Morgan, climbed out of his car and clobbered him. He was fortunate to survive a high-speed flip at Zandvoort when his roll hoop snapped. He earned the moniker 'Hunt the Shunt' as the racing became ever more hair-raising.

It was in Formula 3 in 1970 that Hunt and Lauda first encountered each other, becoming friends. Unusually, they sat down and spoke about the dangers after a particularly wild race.

"Racing drivers never talk among themselves about death," James said, "but that night in Sweden I did discuss it with Niki. We came to a practical rather than philosophical conclusion. We both realized that because of the game we'd chosen, there was really no point in leaving celebrations until later. The chances were pretty high that we'd both get killed. We decided then and there that we'd celebrate as we went along!"

They even shared a London flat for a while and Lauda called Hunt, "an open, honest-to-God pal." With Niki back living on his own, James even remembered his birthday and treated him to a night on the town.

Lauda's logical approach to escaping the harum-scarum of slipstreamer F3 was to go into F2, which he did in 1971 with the aid of an £8,000 sponsorship investment from the Austrian Erste Bank. He did well enough for March directors Max Mosley and Robin Herd to offer him a works deal for F1 and F2 in 1972, provided he could bring around £125,000 sponsorship.

"A bank director cleared me to do the deal, so I signed a contract with Max and Robin. But then the guy said that such a sum of money needed the approval of the supervisory board. My grandfather, Hans Lauda (President of the Federation of Austrian Industries) was on that board and he vetoed it. I telephoned him and asked if he could please fuck off interfering in my business. He said that no, he wouldn't, and that Laudas should be on the business pages of papers, not the sports pages. I never spoke another word to him for the rest of his life." ('Old Lauda' as Hans was known, died in January 1974, aged 77 just before Niki won his first grand prix in a Ferrari.)

Now in a financial hole, Lauda persuaded the rival Raiffeisenkasse bank to grant him a five-year, interest-free loan for the March money, secured against a life insurance policy with their branding on his cars and helmet.

When, at the end of 1972, Mosley told Lauda that March had no money and there was no drive for 1973, the situation looked dire. Lauda approached BRM and took the boss, Louis Stanley, to meet his bank. They didn't speak each other's language, so Lauda controlled the meeting. He started driving for BRM in 1973 on the understanding that his 'sponsorship' was delayed but coming. It wasn't.

The early 1973 season aboard BRM's V12-powered P160 saved him. Lauda finished a promising fifth in the Belgian Grand Prix at

Opposite Lauda's March in the '72 Belgian GP at Nivelles.

Left Hunt aboard his Hesketh-entered March at the Watkins Glen US GP of '73, a race in which he finished second to Ronnie Peterson, just over half a second behind.

Below Hunt broke his F1 duck by beating Lauda's Ferrari to the line in the '75 Dutch GP at Zandvoort.

Above Lauda and Hunt in conversation at Zandvoort in '73.

Right Hunt celebrates a second Dutch GP win with McLaren in '76.

Opposite Hunt's McLaren about to get airborne as the Ferraris of Lauda and Clay Regazzoni touch ahead of him on the opening lap of the British GP at Brands Hatch in '76. James would later win the restarted race, only to be disqualified.

Zolder, then qualified sixth at Monaco and ran a superb third, ahead of Jacky Ickx's Ferrari, before the car's gearbox expired.

That night, with his sponsor payment due, Stanley told Lauda that he no longer needed to pay to drive if he would sign a three-year contract. Niki signed. But, after watching Monaco on TV, Enzo Ferrari had been on the phone to Lauda's Salzburg office. Ferrari had just signed Lauda's BRM teammate Clay Regazzoni, who Niki was outperforming, for 1974, and Clay had put in a good word. Niki told Enzo that he'd just signed a three-year deal with BRM. Ferrari told him not to worry, they'd sort it, clear his debts and pay him a million Austrian Schillings (around £25,000 at the time). He was on his way.

So too was Hunt. When a 1973 works March F3 deal fell apart, James joined forces with Lord Hesketh's team. 'The Good Lord' as James called him, wasn't doing things by halves and took the plunge into Formula 2. Hunt caused a stir by putting the car on the front row for his first race at the Salzburgring. When he finished on the podium at Oulton Park, Hesketh thought, 'Why not go into F1?'

In those days, Formula 1 teams were not required to be constructors, or to compete in all races, and so the flamboyant Hesketh, with his band of Hooray Henrys as the rest of the F1 paddock rather disparagingly viewed them, turned up at Monaco in 1973 with a hired March, where James finished ninth. Anyone looking beyond the superficial dazzle of a team yacht, Jet Ranger helicopter, pin-striped Rolls Royce, champagne and caviar, could see that Hunt could drive. He scored a point for sixth place next time out at Paul Ricard and was a fine fourth in the British Grand Prix at Silverstone.

At Zandvoort he scored his first podium, behind the Tyrrells of Jackie Stewart and François Cevert, but there was little joy in it as the race claimed the life of former F3 rival, the talented Roger Williamson.

In an even better performance, he harried Ronnie Peterson's Lotus all the way to the chequered flag to finish runner-up in the season-closing US Grand Prix. It was another race soured by tragedy after the popular François Cevert had died in a horrible accident during practice and teammate Jackie Stewart had called time on his F1 career there and then.

Whereas the slightly built, buck-toothed Lauda was hardly box office, the tall, athletic, good-looking Hunt, with his aristocratic bearing, mop of blond hair, clear diction, boundless energy and insatiable appetite for cigarettes, beer and women, clearly was.

By 1974, Lauda had joined the ranks of grand prix winners, taking victory in the Spanish GP at Jarama and the Dutch GP at Zandvoort in his first season with Ferrari. Hunt, meanwhile, had driven his 1973 Hesketh season on a £2,500 retainer and 45% of the prize money. For 1974 his retainer was upped to £15,000 as Lord Hesketh invested £200k in a season that saw the respected Harvey Postlethwaite design the team's own car.

James scored podiums in Sweden, where he scrabbled past Niki's Ferrari, in Austria and in another great performance at Watkins Glen in the USA, where he qualified on the front row. That race was the only other title showdown, other than Hamilton versus Verstappen in 2021, in which the protagonists (McLaren's Emerson Fittipaldi and Lauda's Ferrari teammate Regazzoni) started the final race level on points. Fittipaldi took the crown but once again

Right Hunt, leading McLaren
teammate Jochen Mass, clinched an
epic 1976 championship, subject of
the 2013 film *Rush*, in Japan. When the
race began in awful wet and misty
conditions, the looming Mount Fuji
could not even be seen. Title rival
Lauda, unable to blink and properly
clear water from his eyes, retired after
the opening lap, surrendering his title
to Hunt by just a single point after one
of sport's bravest comebacks.

'The Glen' was marred by tragedy as young Austrian Helmuth Koinigg, a friend of Niki's, was decapitated in just his second GP as the Armco barrier parted after a relatively slow-speed impact. 'The Lauda System,' as Niki liked to call it, referred to the way in which he compartmentalized every aspect of his life so that pragmatism and logic dictated his every action, with emotion not permitted to intervene. Now, he needed it.

For 1975, equipped with the new transverse gearbox Ferrari 312T and eliminating some of the impetuous mistakes he'd made the previous season, when he took nine poles from 15 races, Lauda was an unstoppable force. He won five times and sealed Ferrari's first driver's title since John Surtees in 1964 at, of all places, Monza.

That same season, Hunt won his first grand prix with a fabulous Lauda-resisting drive at Zandvoort. Hesketh was the first privateer team to win a race since Rob Walker's team with Jo Siffert at Brands Hatch seven years earlier. But now he had lost his sponsor. 'The Good Lord' had run out of money for his F1 project. Despite finishing fourth in the World Championship behind Lauda, Fittipaldi and Reutemann, Hunt had no seat for 1976.

Fortune smiled upon him. After two seasons at McLaren, two-time champion Emerson Fittipaldi surprised the team by announcing that he was leaving to set up his own operation with brother Wilson and backing from the Brazilian sugar company, Copersucar. A couple of hours before he let his Marlboro McLaren team principal Teddy Mayer know, Emerson had phoned James.

Despite some at McLaren having reservations about hiring a rule-intolerant playboy, seldom had a team and driver needed each other quite so badly. A £45,000 retainer was soon agreed but

James nearly blew it because he didn't like a clause that any Marlboro-sponsored driver at functions should be in blazer, shirt, tie and tailored flannels. The man in control of the Marlboro purse strings, John Hogan, was already a friend, and had to take Hunt quietly aside and explain that he would never, in fact, force him to wear a blazer, but if James didn't sign the contract, the deal was off. Hunt signed and, predictably, continued to charm the world's movers and shakers in his t-shirt, jeans and flip-flops – and he did smoke the product …

To McLaren's great relief, Hunt's speed was obvious from the start and he took pole for the first two races, in Brazil and South Africa. Lauda beat him on Sunday, however, with James retiring at Interlagos and finishing just behind the Ferrari at Kyalami.

At Maranello, Lauda had enjoyed a strong relationship with Luca di Montezemolo, effectively the filter between the dictatorial Enzo and his plain-speaking driver. When, early on, Niki said, "the car is shit," Luca would always couch it in more diplomatic terms. But now, Montezemolo was being fast-tracked elsewhere in the FIAT/Ferrari empire and Lauda was unsure about his replacement, Daniele Audetto.

Audetto liked society dinners while Niki had no time for them, so started to gravitate more towards his teammate Regazzoni, an Italian-speaking Swiss. When Audetto approached Lauda ahead of round three at Long Beach and suggested that it was time that Clay won a race, Niki gave him short shrift. In his mind he figured that at year-end, either he or Audetto would have to go.

At this early stage of the season, Ferrari was perhaps underestimating the potential threat from Hunt and McLaren.

Opposite Lauda, carrying the World Champion's No.1, started the '76 season and his title defence by winning the first two races with Ferrari's 312T.

Above Lauda, driving with a corset and pain-killing injections after rolling a tractor at his home, led the Spanish GP at Jarama until Hunt forced past. Hunt's McLaren was then disqualified for being too wide, but reinstated a couple of months later.

Left Lauda leads Ferrari teammate Regazzoni in France on the way to his first world title in '75.

As it happened, Regazzoni did win at Long Beach because Niki had car problems and could only finish second. Hunt collided with Patrick Depailler and, for some considerable time, stood in the middle of the track shaking his fist at the Frenchman every time he went by. Not content with that, he strode into the post-race press conference after Patrick finished third, and had a wild rant at the Frenchman.

Shortly afterwards, Lauda was fortunate to escape with a couple of broken ribs when he turned a tractor over while working on an earth bank at home in Vienna. Showing his characteristic determination, he raced in the Spanish GP with a corset and pain-killing injections, leading the race for 30 laps before pole man Hunt barged past. But, at post-race scrutineering, the McLaren was found to be 1.8mm too wide and James was disqualified.

When Lauda won back-to-back races in Belgium and Monaco, and finished third in Sweden while Hunt posted three retirements, the contest appeared over. With the season approaching the halfway point in France, the score (9-6-4-3-2-1 to the first six finishers) was: Lauda, 55 points; Hunt, 8.

But then the pendulum swung dramatically. James took pole and won the French GP at Paul Ricard while Niki suffered a rare Ferrari engine failure while leading. And, prior to the British GP at Brands Hatch, McLaren's appeal against Hunt's Spanish GP disqualification was upheld.

Lauda took pole at Brands Hatch but was clipped by teammate Regazzoni at the first corner. In attempted avoidance Hunt's McLaren was tipped up onto two wheels, breaking a steering arm, and with cars blocking the track, the race was red-flagged.

Hunt abandoned his damaged race car close to a back road behind the pits and returned on foot.

James and Regazzoni were strapped into their respective spare cars. The rules, however, said that spares could not be used once a race had started. The capacity crowd, amid the UK's long hot summer of 1976, was unamused. Apples, empty beer cans, then full beer cans were lobbed onto the track as the atmosphere became ugly. As arguments with race officials continued, McLaren mechanics worked feverishly to fix Hunt's race car. Technically though, it should not have been allowed to start. Hunt did start, shadowed Lauda for 44 laps, then dived past and went on to score a dominant win. The score was now Lauda, 58; Hunt 35.

Nürburgring was next. Lauda, criticized and called 'chicken' in Germany for his view that the daunting 14-mile Nordschleife was no longer safe for F1 and should be boycotted, had only the previous year set the first sub-7 minute lap of 'The Ring' when his Ferrari took pole with 6 minutes 58.6 seconds. This time, James beat him to pole. On a slippery but drying track, all bar Hunt's teammate Jochen Mass started on wet tyres and changed to slicks after the opening lap. Lauda lost it midway around the following lap and was hit by two following cars as the Ferrari's ruptured fuel tank caught fire.

He was rescued from the burning Ferrari by Guy Edwards, Harald Ertl, Brett Lunger and Arturo Merzario, a former Ferrari driver who was familiar with Lauda's seatbelt harness. Badly burned with scorched lungs damaged by toxic fumes from the burning Ferrari bodywork, Lauda's life hung in the balance for a week, during which he was administered the last rites. Hunt won the restarted

German race to close to within 14 points of Lauda's championship lead. Surely, now, the championship was a formality for James?

But that was counting without the spirit and sheer guts of Niki Lauda. After John Watson won his first grand prix in Austria, where Hunt was fourth, James won at Zandvoort and went to Monza just two points behind Lauda. But, miraculously, just 39 days after the accident, Lauda had tested his Ferrari and planned to drive in the Italian GP.

There were political machinations at play, too. Both McLarens and Watson's Penske were found to have fuel of too high an octane after samples were taken on Saturday and had to take their (wet) Friday times for the grid, which meant that they didn't qualify. They were only permitted to start after three other drivers stood down. The wound-up Hunt slid into a chicane gravel trap early on.

Despite Enzo Ferrari signing Reutemann from Brabham for 1977 while Lauda was still in hospital, much to Niki's disgust, and entering the Argentine in a third car at Monza, Lauda was the quickest Ferrari qualifier, fifth, and went on to finish a heroic fourth, his balaclava caked in blood from his Nürburgring burns.

"His race speaks for itself," Hunt said. "To virtually step out of the grave and six weeks later come fourth in a Grand Prix is a truly amazing achievement."

It was now 61–56 with three races remaining but that gap was about to grow. While playing squash in Toronto ahead of the Canadian GP, Hunt discovered that a six-man jury at an FIA Court of Appeal in Paris had upheld Ferrari's appeal against his British GP win. James lost his nine points; Niki gained a further three and suddenly it was 64–47, which looked insurmountable.

McLaren's Alistair Caldwell said that the court had been influenced by a surprise Ferrari witness – one N. Lauda, with a bloodied bandage on his head.

"It was long after his wounds had healed," the straight-talking Caldwell said. "The little p**** was as bouncy and fit as a jack rabbit. He didn't need any bandages. But it worked. The silly old sods who did the deciding decided that it was unfair on poor Niki."

Temporarily, it looked as if the relationship between the two drivers had broken down. Lauda professed himself "madly delighted" at the court verdict, which angered Hunt. Both were on the GPDA safety committee and when Niki asked James to attend a meeting to discuss Mosport's safety, James's retort was, "To hell with safety. All I want to do is race."

Lauda realized Hunt was disgruntled about Brands Hatch but had no sympathy: "We've been friends but James broke the rules in England. If you break the rules you are out. No argument. Now he shouts at me. That's not right. He should respect me as a driver. We have a job to do. Bad feeling only makes it more difficult."

The media, of course, stirred it for all it was worth but Hunt later claimed that it was only gamesmanship, trying to get into Niki's head and make him wary on-track of a James in that frame of mind. Make him easier to overtake!

Off-track, Hunt indulged his liking for drink and women with a vengeance, even the night before the race, something he wouldn't normally do. Caldwell, believing the championship was gone, didn't stop him.

But, from pole position, despite a serious hangover, Hunt completely controlled the Canadian GP while Lauda, struggling

with tyre temperature, could only finish eighth and failed to score. The gap was back to eight points with two races to go.

Both men realized they were being played by the press, shook hands and continued their good relationship. A week later at Watkins Glen they even had adjoining hotel rooms and left their doors open in the evening and socialized together.

On race day, Hunt had his morning call booked for 8am so that he could be at the track an hour later. Knowing that, Lauda barged in at 7am fully suited up and, stood to attention at the bottom of Hunt's bed, declaring, "Today I vin ze championship!" James thought it was hilarious.

Niki didn't win it, though. Hunt did it again, winning from pole with Scheckter the only driver remotely in touch. Lauda managed third place meaning that he went to the season finale in Japan three points in front. But Hunt had an extra win. If James won at Fuji, he was champion.

The late October weather was predictably awful. The race should never really have started but with worldwide interest in the showdown, TV companies had booked satellite time and the Japanese fans had paid their money. Neither James nor Niki thought they should be driving but, an hour and a half late, the five-minute starting signal was given.

Hunt splashed off into the lead from second on the grid behind pole man Mario Andretti, while Lauda, who started third, dropped to the back and pulled disconsolately in at the end of the opening lap. The fear had returned, visibility was virtually zero and his position was made worse by being unable to blink away tears due to operations on his burned eyelids. "Some things are more

Opposite Things would get spiky when Hunt and Mario Andretti collided in the '77 Dutch GP at Zandvoort.

Above Lauda's Ferrari leads Andretti in the same race before the Lotus retired and Lauda's victory set him on the way to a second world title.

Right Formula 1 impresario Bernie Ecclestone with his box office draw, Hunt, ahead of the '77 Swedish GP at Anderstorp.

Below Hunt berated Frenchman Patrick Depailler after his McLaren was launched at the first corner of the US GP West at Long Beach in '77.

Opposite Six years after Hunt's F1 debut at Monaco in 1973, he'd had enough. Driving for Walter Wolf in '79, he quit the sport with immediate effect seven races into the '79 season, after six retirements.

important than the World Championship," he said. Fittipaldi, Carlos Pace and Larry Perkins had reached the same conclusion and also stopped.

Hunt saw 'NIKI OUT' on his pitboard and knew that third place would be enough, but continued to lead. As the race developed and the track dried, conservation of the wet rubber became key and while second-placed Andretti was seeking out the puddles, James was not responding to 'COOL TYRES' messages on his pitboard.

The team wanted James to make the call on when to stop as he was the one driving; James wanted the team to make the call as they had more information on the tyres from other cars. He ploughed on until the left front, down to the canvas, let go and forced him into the pits. The car needed physically lifting to get the new tyres on and his stop took 27 agonizing seconds.

Hunt blasted back into the race not knowing where he was or what he had to do. He pulled off outside overtakes on Alan Jones and Clay Regazzoni with two laps to go and crossed the line behind Andretti (a lap ahead still on his starting set of wets) and Depailler.

Coming into the pitlane, Hunt was convinced his team had cost him the championship and was standing up in the cockpit berating team principal Teddy Mayer before it could be got through to him that he was in fact third and the new World Champion. Lauda, meanwhile, was already at the airport. Formula 1 was on TV to stay and its best season thus far was at an end.

"It's a shame we couldn't share the championship," James said.

"If I couldn't win it, I'm pleased James has," said Niki.

The following season, Lauda regained his title with three wins and calculating drives before leaving Ferrari for Bernie Ecclestone's Brabham team.

Hunt, increasingly aware and fearful of the dangers, endured tougher seasons with McLaren in 1977–8 before accepting a $1 million offer to drive for Walter Wolf in 1979. He had been deeply affected by the death of Ronnie Peterson following a startline accident at Monza in 1978 and, when the Wolf proved uncompetitive, he abruptly quit racing after the 1979 Monaco Grand Prix.

Four months later, Lauda was gone too, "fed up with driving around in circles" after his V12 Alfa-powered Brabham BT48 proved unreliable.

After a break of two years in which he concentrated on his airline business, Lauda Air, he was tempted back to F1 by McLaren in 1982, by which time he needed extra money to invest in his business. In 1984 he beat McLaren teammate Alain Prost by half a point to clinch a third world title.

Hunt later fought inner demons and depression and became known for a no-holds-barred F1 commentary style in partnership with Murray Walker, often attacking Riccardo Patrese who he blamed for triggering the accident that killed his friend Ronnie Peterson. He succumbed to a massive heart attack in June 1993, aged just 45.

Jones vs. Piquet

Jones
12 Grand Prix wins
1 Championship

Piquet
23 Grand Prix wins
3 Championships

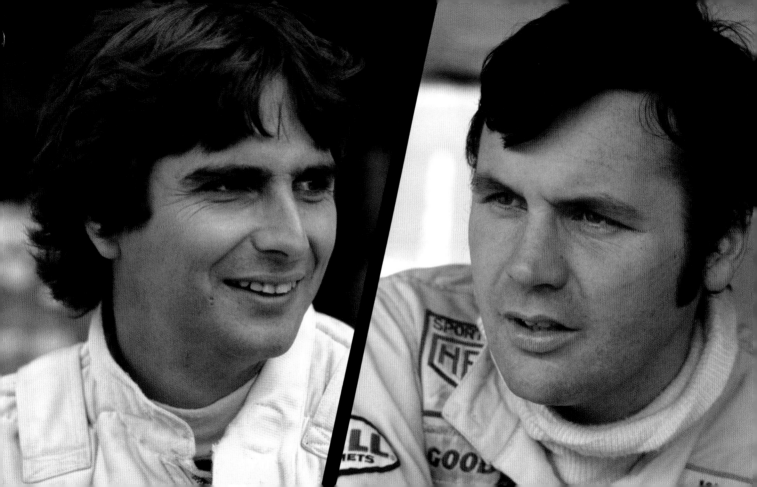

Opposite Nelson Piquet joined Bernie Ecclestone's Brabham team in 1978 after winning the British F3 title.

Right Alan Jones in the Embassy Hill at Nürburgring in 1975.

Alan Jones ('AJ'), born 2 November 1946, is a straight-talking, no-nonsense Australian, son of Stan Jones, himself a successful racing driver-turned-motor trader. Stan won the non-championship 1959 Australian Grand Prix in a Maserati 250F and regarded himself in triple World Champion Jack Brabham's league, although he never ventured to Europe. He died in 1973, aged just 50, after two strokes.

In the good years, before Stan's Melbourne dealerships went bankrupt, Alan had a privileged life: private school, holidays on the Gold Coast, karting, then racing. But, by the time he headed to Europe with long-time family friend Brian McGuire (killed at Brands Hatch in 1977), he had to do it all on his own.

They sold Dormobiles to travelling Aussies in Earls Court, doing well enough to put down money on Formula 3 cars. Alan and wife Bev would rent a five-bedroom house, telling agents they had a big family in Australia who liked to have their own bedrooms when they came over. They then filled the rooms with bunk beds and found B&B guests. Alan made breakfasts and then concentrated on furthering his racing ambitions.

He won 10 F3 races across the 1973–4 seasons before Formula Atlantic entrant Harry Stiller decided he was going into F1 and that in 1975 Alan would drive for him in a customer Hesketh 308 – the same car in which James Hunt had started making his name the previous season. That was until, according to Jones, Stiller suddenly upped sticks and left for the USA – something to do with the tax man.

At the same time, an awful crash in Montjuïc Park – in which Spanish Grand Prix spectators died – injured Rolf Stommelen. Graham Hill's new Embassy-sponsored F1 team needed a driver and Jones found himself drafted in for four races and managed a fifth place at the Nürburgring.

While respectful of Hill's racing achievements, Jones had his enthusiasm for his boss well under control. He could easily have been at the ill-fated Paul Ricard test in November 1975, returning from which Hill crashed his private plane, killing himself, promising driver Tony Brise and four crew members.

In his biography, Jones says candidly, "Graham asked me to come back and test their new car at Ricard but changed his mind. Only a few weeks after, he took Brise down there instead.

"I wasn't surprised Graham died in a plane crash. I'm not saying anything about the cause of the crash, but he was a shit pilot. He didn't concentrate. Numerous times with him I feared for my life. But Graham gave me a drive and I'm grateful for that … At Embassy Hill, if you could keep Graham away, you could get somewhere."

Alan then went from the team of one British World Champion to another – that of John Surtees. Of Surtees, he added, "I had a very fraught time driving for Big John. He was like Graham in that he thought he knew everything there was to know about racing; he presumed that because I was relatively new to the championship, I knew nothing. Every time I changed gear I scraped the skin off my knuckles. I asked John to put a bubble on the side of the cockpit but he wouldn't do it: he thought it would look funny if there wasn't a bubble on the other side. It just wouldn't look symmetrical. Damn the symmetry, I just wanted to be able to change gear without coming away bleeding …"

For 1977, he left behind the frustration and anger of his years with Hill and Surtees and joined Shadow. Alan Jones was always

good in the wet and at a soaking Österreichring, won the Austrian Grand Prix from 14th on the grid. He ended up seventh in the championship with 22 of Shadow's 23 points.

The Aussie then came close to a Ferrari drive but for marketing reasons the Scuderia wanted a North American alongside Niki Lauda. When Mario Andretti opted for Lotus, they took Gilles Villeneuve. Jones then went to meet Frank Williams and Patrick Head, who were planning a one-car team in 1978 with their neat FW06, ahead of a two-car ground effect effort in 1979, with Saudi Arabian backing.

"Frank deserved everything he got," Jones recalls. "He was the best bloke I ever drove for; a really nice guy." Jones and technical director Head also gelled, Patrick appreciating the toughness, the effort and the pertinent feedback that allowed him to get on with engineering while Alan got on with driving.

Meanwhile, Nelson Piquet Souto Maior, born 17 August 1952, was one of a succession of Brazilians who blazed the same successful trail, inspired by Emerson Fittipaldi, who won world titles with Lotus in 1972 and McLaren in 1974. After a brief dalliance with the idea of becoming a tennis professional, he shortened his name from Souto Maior to Piquet to prevent his father from learning about his motorsport activities. He became a successful karter and Formula Super Vee driver in Brazil. In 1977 Nelson made the move to Europe and won a couple of European Formula 3 rounds before launching a full onslaught on the two British F3 series the following year. He put himself on the F1 radar when he won 13 times in 27 starts and claimed the BP championship while chief rival, Britain's Derek Warwick, narrowly took the Vandervell series.

Ensign team boss Mo Nunn gave Piquet his F1 debut that same 1978 season in the German GP, before Nelson drove a privately entered McLaren M23 in Austria, Holland and Italy. One man paying close attention to his performances was Bernie Ecclestone, who offered a drive in a third Brabham-Alfa alongside Niki Lauda and John Watson in the Canadian Grand Prix. With Watson moving to McLaren for 1979, Nelson did enough to earn himself a full-time seat alongside Lauda.

With ground effect aerodynamics the key development in F1 at the time, Vee rather than flat engine configurations optimized downforce, but Brabham engine partner Alfa Romeo's V12 was heavy and thirsty. Typically, Lauda and Piquet would qualify near the front and then go backwards with a full tank of fuel and greater tyre wear. Reliability was woeful and by the end of September, Lauda, "fed up with driving around in circles," stepped out of his car during Canadian Grand Prix practice and walked away from the sport.

Jones wryly observed that Niki had enjoyed the advantage of 12-cylinder power during most of his F1 career, whether that be at BRM, Ferrari or Brabham and, faced with a Cosworth V8-powered car – the direction Brabham was going – and the challenge of the young, hungry Piquet, he had seen the writing on the wall and elected to preserve his market value. Lauda did indeed return to F1, just over two years later.

Piquet stepped capably into the team leader role and established a great rapport with Ecclestone, visionary designer Gordon Murray and his Brabham team. Future FIA race director Charlie Whiting and deputy Herbie Blash worked on Nelson's

Opposite Piquet in the Brabham BT46, Argentina '79.

Left Nelson prepares for the '79 US GP West.

Below The switch from the Alfa V12-powered Brabham BT48 to the lighter Cosworth-powered BT49 transformed Piquet into a front-runner at the end of '79. He is pictured in front of Elio de Angelis's Shadow at Watkins Glen in the US, where he qualified on the front row.

car and it was a happy band of brothers as Nelson contended for the 1980 World Championship.

His principal rival was Jones. The ground effect Williams FW07 of 1979 was a revelation and at Zolder in Belgium, Alan qualified fourth, his best-ever qualifying position. Between the French and British grands prix, Williams aero chief Frank Dernie corrected some aero leakage at the back of the car and ensured that the all-important side skirts stayed in contact with the ground. Suddenly the FW07 wasn't just good, it was a rocket ship. Jones dominated Silverstone qualifying, putting the car on pole and leading the race until a water pump broke, whereupon teammate Clay Regazzoni scored Williams' first grand prix win. In Germany, Jones made amends to secure a win, then went on to achieve a hat-trick with wins in Austria and Holland.

He then had to drive with pain-killing injections for a couple of races after an altercation, to quote Alan, "with some large gentlemen (in a van) in the Chiswick High Road at around midnight …" which left him with a broken finger and multiple bruising. The story that he'd been bitten by a scooter on a zebra crossing didn't wash with wife Bev and Frank was none too impressed. The scoring system that year included only a driver's best four scores from the first half of the season and his best four from the second. All Jones could call on from the first half was a lone third place, allowing Jody Scheckter and Ferrari to take the titles. For 1980 though, Jones and Williams would start favourites.

After Alan won the season-opener in Argentina, Nelson hit back with an accomplished win in round four at Long Beach.

Jones won back-to-back races at Paul Ricard and Silverstone, then Piquet did likewise at Zandvoort and Imola, after which the championship score was: Piquet, 54 points; Jones 53, with just the North American rounds at Montreal and Watkins Glen remaining.

In Canada, Jones felt confident and was quicker for most of the practices, but then Piquet outqualified him by almost a full second. Jones was unfazed, believing that Nelson's engine was a 'qualifying special' (in the days when teams could bring built-up spare cars and qualifying engines) that could not last the distance in the race.

Both starting from the front row, they made contact in what was then a first turn right-hand kink in Montreal. Nelson believed Alan had squeezed him, with pandemonium behind in avoidance leading to a race stoppage. The Williams was undamaged but Piquet needed to restart in the spare Brabham, still fitted with the qualifying special …

Jones again led off the start, with Didier Pironi's Ligier also beating Piquet away. With his powerful engine, however, Piquet was rapidly past both and into the lead. But he knew it was a long-shot that the engine would last. And it didn't … The complexities of the scoring system, where five of the first seven races and five of the second eight counted, meant that Jones's race gave him the championship and Williams took its first of nine Constructors-Championships.

Piquet and Jones were again the major contenders in 1981, joined this time by Alan's new Williams teammate, the enigmatic Carlos Reutemann. The Argentinian could be in inspirational form one day and lacklustre the next and team boss Frank Williams

Opposite Jones's season with Shadow in '77 put him on the map. Seen here at Long Beach, he went on to win a wet Austrian GP.

Above Jones, leading Mario Andretti's Lotus at Anderstorp, '78, turned in a number of impressive drives with the Williams FW06.

Left Jones and Williams teammate Carlos Reutemann ahead of the 1980 South African GP at Kyalami.

Left Piquet and Jean-Pierre Jabouille's Renault fight for the lead of the 1980 Dutch GP at Zandvoort.

Opposite Alan Jones signed off his Williams career with a dominant win in the 1981 Las Vegas GP, a race which brought Piquet (running fifth on the opening lap for Brabham) his first World Championship title.

Right Race winner Alan Jones and new World Champion Nelson Piquet celebrate after the 1981 United States Grand Prix.

was never sure which Carlos he was going to get. Jones and Reutemann fell out in the second race, the Brazilian GP in Rio, after Carlos ignored a pit instruction to move over and let Williams team leader Jones take the win.

Jones and Piquet clashed in the Belgium Grand Prix at Zolder in a controversial race where the starting procedure was thrown into chaos after Piquet missed his grid slot and was sent round for another lap. With the cars on the grid overheating as they waited for the Brabham to return, some turned their engines off. A mechanic stranded on the grid trying to restart Riccardo Patrese's Arrows was hit when the race started.

In the early stages of the grand prix Jones went down Piquet's inside and nudged Nelson off into some catch fencing. A few laps later, a gearbox failure in the Williams sent Jones careering into the barriers, with his left thigh badly burned after hot gearbox oil leaked into the cockpit. Following Jones's retirement, a furious Piquet stormed down to the Williams pit and stated that he'd put Jones "over the fence" if that happened again. It was suggested to Nelson that given their respective builds, it was probably in his best interests not to go looking for Alan. At the following race in Monaco, with Piquet leading, Jones bullied him into the barriers.

Jones book-ended 1981 with victories at the season-opener at Long Beach and the finale in a Caesars Palace car park in Las Vegas, but failed to win in between. It was teammate Reutemann who battled Piquet in the Vegas shoot-out. Asked before the race if he wanted Carlos or Nelson to win the World Championship he allegedly said: "It's take your pick between TB and cancer. I couldn't give a damn."

Reutemann started from pole but slowly faded with an ill-handing car. Piquet badly bruised his shoulder against the side of the cockpit in the early stages, but on lap 16 passed his rival for the points he needed. Later in the race Piquet was sick in his helmet and needed to be lifted from his car after the chequered flag. On the point of collapse, the Brazilian only just managed to lift the trophy at the ceremony.

That there was no love lost between Jones and Piquet was never a secret. "We didn't get on, I didn't like him," Jones states. "We never saw eye to eye. I think he was rude and unnecessarily undiplomatic. His best skill was getting himself into the best cars. I thought he was a tool as a person, but he was a bloody good driver."

Jones's retirement at the end of the 1981 season came as a big surprise to Frank Williams, who was only informed of the decision three races before the end. "Alan's departure so late in the season, besides being grossly inconsiderate to us, was a big setback for our plans," he told Nigel Roebuck. "By the time he'd told me he was stopping there was no one of his calibre – Villeneuve or Pironi or Prost or Piquet – available. They'd all done deals elsewhere."

There was a half-hearted return in 1985/86 with a Team Haas Lola that yielded four championship points over 20 races and more retirements than finishes. Piquet would continue racing until 1991, becoming champion again in 1983, and rather more fortuitously in 1987. But that's another story.

Villeneuve vs. Pironi

Villeneuve
6 Grand Prix wins
0 Championships

Pironi
3 Grand Prix wins
0 Championships

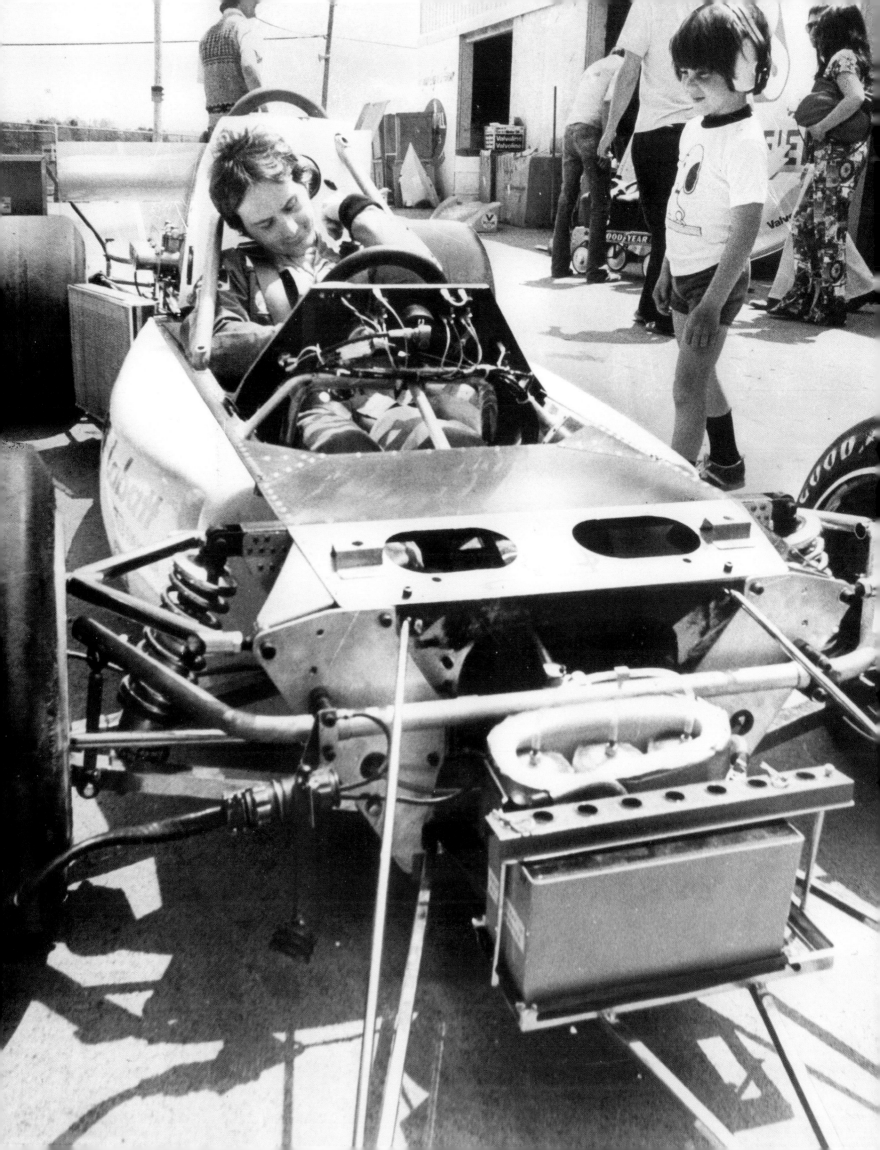

Gilles Villeneuve was one of Ferrari's most revered drivers. Born on 18 January 1950 in Saint-Jean-Sur-Richelieu close to Montreal, he was two years older than he admitted while racing, having started late. He was the son of a piano tuner father who had a penchant for fast driving on local roads and would sit a young Gilles on his knee and let him steer.

The family moved to Berthierville, where a museum dedicated to Gilles can now be found. His first experience of circuit racing was a trip to St Jovite to see a mix of saloons and Formula Ford/Formula Vee single-seaters.

"It all looked completely inaccessible to me," he told biographer Gerald Donaldson. "The cars cost so much money. But I figured that about 90% of the drivers were wankers. I thought I could do better."

About 30 years earlier a fellow Quebecois, Armand Bombardier, had invented the snowmobile and when his father bought one, Gilles was soon entering local races. Despite his slight stature and baby face, Villeneuve's bravery and balance saw him become an immediate race winner.

His long-suffering girlfriend and soon wife, Joann, found herself spending all day freezing at snowmobile races, especially when Gilles was hired by the Skiroule factory as a driver/mechanic and actually started earning money doing something he hugely enjoyed. With son Jacques born in 1971, when Gilles was just 21, and his Skiroule drive stopping, he raced on as a privateer with the prize money from winter racing the Villeneuve family's only income. A friend, however, suggested that the skills that made him Canadian snowmobile champion might translate to cars

once the snow melted. He was pointed in the direction of the Jim Russell racing school at Mont Tremblant.

Gilles was soon winning races in Formula Ford and the family, now augmented by the arrival of daughter Melanie, became racing gypsies, travelling from race to race, summer and winter. Gilles sold their static mobile home to put a deposit on a Formula Atlantic drive in which he had minor successes but suffered from underfunding.

It wasn't until the 1975 end-of-season, non-championship Molson GP that he could match himself against a number of top European drivers. Also competing was Vittorio Brambilla, who had just won the Austrian GP with March, as well as Shadow's Jean-Pierre Jarier and Tyrrell's Patrick Depailler. Gilles qualified third, right behind Jarier and Depailler, who he immediately overtook. He was pushing Jarier hard until his brakes failed.

Skiroule agreed to back Gilles in Atlantic in 1976, and now he started to clean up, that is, until Skiroule went bankrupt. Suddenly, despite leading the championship, there was no money. After sitting out one race, Gilles was introduced to Montreal entrepreneur Gaston Parent.

"He looked about 17 (Gilles was now 26), a bit shy and nervous, constantly rubbing his hands together," Parent recalled, "But he was animated when he talked about racing with real conviction. He said he could win the Canadian championship easily, and also the American title and the Trois-Rivières race. Nothing could stop him. Except the lack of $5,000,…"

Parent stumped up the cash and ended up a close friend and manager. Gilles did everything he'd promised and it was the Trois-Rivières race that made his name. This time the visiting European stars included James Hunt, then fighting for the F1 World Championship with Niki Lauda.

Hunt was being paid $10,000 appearance money and was in identical equipment and the same Ecurie Canada team as Gilles, as was Depailler again. But neither James nor Patrick could get anywhere near him. To his eternal credit, Hunt returned to Europe and told McLaren boss Teddy Mayer, "I've just been blown off by this kid called Villeneuve. He's magic. You really ought to get hold of him."

Mayer did so and soon, Villeneuve and Parent found themselves in a meeting with Mayer and Marlboro's sponsorship guru, John Hogan. In return for a $25,000 signing fee, McLaren could run a third car for Gilles alongside Hunt and Jochen Mass in up to five grands prix in 1977 and take an option on him for 1978.

Villeneuve made his F1 debut at Silverstone in 1977. He drove a racing car very much like he drove a snowmobile, sideways and very spectacularly. Veteran Chris Amon, now retired from F1, had driven a CanAm car for Canadian oil entrepreneur and future F1 team owner Walter Wolf and Gilles had guested in the car. Amon said, "I've only known one driver in the world who had the car control Villeneuve has. That was Jimmy Clark."

High praise indeed. But McLaren was somewhat concerned that their rookie's approach to learning Silverstone in a pre-race test was to spin at practically every corner. Gilles was learning the limits by exceeding them, and working back from there. He was so confident in his ability that he was quite happy to spin, knowing he could control the car and wouldn't hit anything.

In the race, in an old McLaren M23 versus the newer M26s of Hunt and Jochen Mass, he qualified ninth, two tenths quicker than the German, then ran seventh before a temperature gauge climbed unhealthily and brought him into the pits. It was a faulty gauge and Gilles lost a couple of laps. He rejoined behind Jody Scheckter, Mario Andretti and Gunnar Nilsson, who were fighting for fourth, and stayed right with them for the remaining 55 laps, setting fifth quickest lap of the race.

He then returned to Canada to drive in an Atlantic race at a track called St Félicien, which is where he encountered Didier Pironi for the first time. The 25-year-old Parisian, a front runner in the European F2 Championship who would make his F1 debut with Ken Tyrrell the following season, was guesting in a Chevron.

Villeneuve was nonplussed when Pironi introduced himself and said that back in Europe, Gilles was being associated with a Ferrari drive and that the team intended to test him against one of Didier's F2 rivals, American Eddie Cheever, for the seat.

Later in the season Gilles was crestfallen when no more McLaren drives materialized and Mayer told him he would not be taking up his option for 1978. Instead, the team had opted for Frenchman Patrick Tambay. Mayer said later, "Gilles looked like he might be a bit expensive (crash prone) and, anyway, Tambay was showing almost the same promise in an Ensign, which wasn't as good as our M23."

But Pironi's tip-off was correct and, just as Gilles was coping with the morale-busting rejection, the phone rang and it was Ferrari. Would he be interested in driving for them? Soon he was being picked up at Milan's Malpensa Airport and driven to an audience with Enzo Ferrari.

Opposite Pironi and Jean-Pierre Jaussaud celebrate their 1978 Le Mans 24 Hours victory for Renault-Alpine in Paris's Place de la Concorde.

Above Gilles Villeneuve made his F1 debut in a third McLaren at the 1977 British GP at Silverstone.

Left Villeneuve aboard Ferrari's 312T3 ahead of the '78 South African GP at Kyalami.

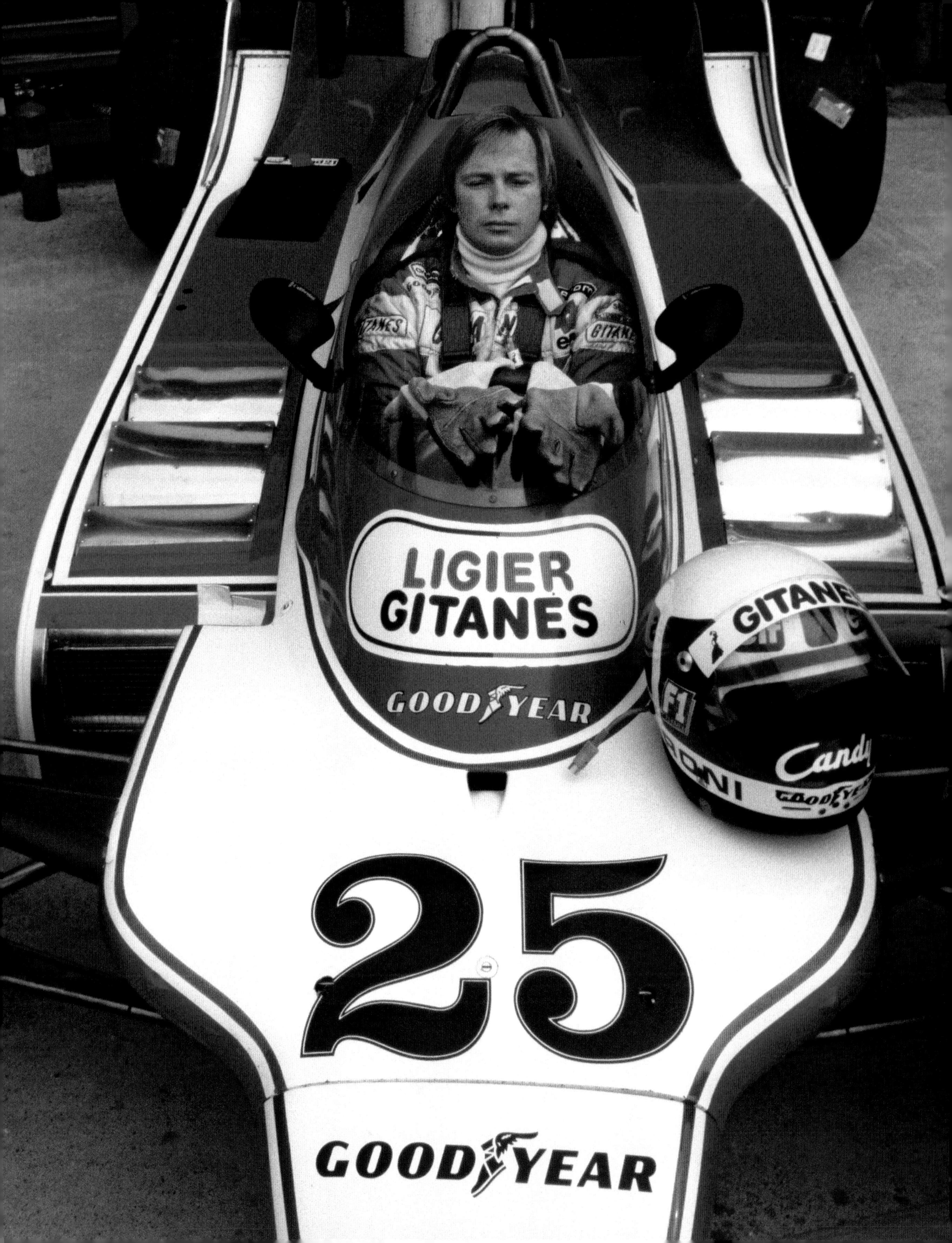
LIGIER
GITANES
GOODYEAR
25
GOODYEAR
GITANES
F1
Candy

After a test at Fiorano, Gilles was back at the end of September to sign a contract, all the while fearing that Ferrari might sign Cheever or Mario Andretti, who they both tested as well. Andretti, though, had opted to go to Lotus, where he would win the championship the following season. Niki Lauda was leaving for Brabham after clinching his second Ferrari world title. But angered by Ferrari's treatment of his loyal mechanic, Ermanno Cuoghi, who was going to Brabham with him the following year, Lauda left with immediate effect. Villeneuve would drive alongside Carlos Reutemann in Canada and Japan for the remaining two races, then partner the Argentine in 1978. The deal to become Ferrari's 71st F1 driver was $75,000 for Gilles, plus 25% of the car (for sponsors), plus $15,000 for the family's travel expenses.

Influential in all this had been Walter Wolf and Chris Amon. Wolf had struck up a friendship with Enzo Ferrari after buying several of his road cars and had even been allowed to test his F1 car at Fiorano. Enzo also had great respect for the opinions of his former driver, Amon. Both men told him that while Gilles was a bit raw and inexperienced, he was brave, hugely enthusiastic and very, very fast. Villeneuve's Ferrari career started inauspiciously. In Canada he spun on oil and then broke a driveshaft with excessive use of the right boot when rejoining. Then, at Mount Fuji, he collided with the back of Ronnie Peterson's Tyrrell, cartwheeled into a group of people standing in a restricted area and killed a 25-year-old amateur photographer and a 21-year-old track marshal, injuring 10 others.

In 1978, the year that Villeneuve and Pironi had their first full F1 seasons, the ground effect Lotus 79s of Andretti and Ronnie Peterson dominated. Reutemann finished third in the championship for Ferrari and Gilles drove some eye-catching races. He was fifth in Belgium, put his Ferrari 312T3 on the front row at Monza and then capped the year with an emotional victory in his home race in Montreal after the leading Lotus retired.

Didier Pironi was born in the Paris suburb of Villecresnes to Italian parents who emigrated to France and established a successful construction business. Influenced by half-brother José Dolhem, who raced, Pironi followed in his footsteps and won a Pilot Elf scholarship in 1972. He was Formule Renault champion in 1974, won the Super Renault series in 1976 and, in 1977, claimed the prestigious Monaco F3 race. That and Ken Tyrrell's association with French petrol company Elf, fast-tracked Didier into the Tyrrell F1 team for 1978, when he also won Le Mans with Alpine Renault.

Although outdriven by the more experienced Patrick Depailler, in much the same way that Villeneuve was by Reutemann at Ferrari, Pironi showed speed and promise and was fifth in Monaco and Germany.

Villeneuve truly emerged in 1979 alongside Jody Scheckter, who had left Walter Wolf's team to replace Reutemann as the Ferrari No.1. Scheckter, wild in his early days, was now experienced and pragmatic and more concerned with winning the championship, making some money and staying alive. He got on famously with his non-political, crazy little French-Canadian teammate, who did everything flat out.

In Ferrari's 312T4, Villeneuve threatened Scheckter for supremacy, winning a hat-trick of early-season races; the

non-championship Race of Champions at Brands Hatch and then grands prix in Scheckter's South African backyard and at Long Beach.

Villeneuve was now a massive draw in F1, hugely spectacular and increasingly acknowledged as the fastest man on the grid. As ground effect cars developed and Ferrari's flat 12 engine configuration proved less than ideal, Gilles's press-on, never-say-die attitude allowed Ferrari to be in the fight and endeared him to spectators the world over. His legendary wheel-banging scrap with Renault's René Arnoux for second place in the French GP, where they were off the circuit everywhere, was seen as irresponsible by some, heroic by others. Defending champion Mario Andretti laughed it off as, "just two young lions clawing each other ..."

Mechanical misfortune meant that Villeneuve was unable to capitalize on his great start to the year, Scheckter hitting back with wins in Belgium and Monaco, so that by the time they went to Monza in September, Jody could clinch the championship. Showing the kind of integrity for which he was known, Gilles, clearly with more speed, sat dutifully behind his Ferrari team leader and followed him across the line as the South African took the title. "I was hoping like hell that he would break ..." Villeneuve admitted. He finished the year runner-up.

Over at Tyrrell, Depailler had left to join Jacques Laffite at Ligier and Pironi became the team's No.1 in 1979, impressing with a couple of podiums, which put him on Guy Ligier's radar. The former French rugby international's Ligier team was now at the front end of the grid and – signed for 1980 – Pironi won his first grand prix with the team at Zolder.

But it was Brands Hatch that shaped Didier's immediate destiny. After taking pole position he led comfortably until a deflating left front sent him into the pits. He produced a scintillating recovery drive, smashing the lap record time and again until he suffered another tyre deflation as the Ligier experienced cracked wheel rims. However, watching behind his dark glasses on TV in Maranello, Enzo Ferrari turned to his advisors and said, "I want Pironi."

The 1980 season was a write-off for Ferrari, hopelessly outclassed by Cosworth V8-powered ground effect cars and its T5 a lemon. A brace of fifths from Gilles and one from Jody as they dropped to 14th and 19th respectively in the championship, prompted Scheckter to hang up his helmet.

Ferrari had been developing a turbo engine and, in 1981, arrived with its 126CK. The engine was potent but to call the chassis agricultural would be offensive to the likes of Massey Ferguson.

Somehow, Villeneuve managed to put the unwieldy car on the front row at Monaco of all places, missing Nelson Piquet's pole position by just 0.07 seconds. By contrast, new teammate Pironi was 17th, almost 2.5 seconds adrift. Piquet led until his car broke, Alan Jones's Williams took over until, in the closing stages, he had a fuel-feed problem. Sniffing half a chance, Villeneuve arrowed his Ferrari tractor between the Williams and the barrier with millimetres to spare to take one of the most unlikely victories of all time.

A fortnight later, at Jarama, he did it again. From seventh on the grid, after a great start, he found himself leading when Jones made a mistake. Gilles headed a five-car train for the entire race without making a single error, 1.25 seconds covering all five cars across the finish line. The designer, Harvey Postlethwaite,

Opposite Pironi in Gerard Ducarouge's attractive and effective Ligier JS11/15, with which he won in Belgium, '80.

Left By 1979, Villeneuve and Ferrari's 312T4 had become F1's most exciting combination.

Below Mauro Forghieri, Villeneuve, Marco Piccinini, Enzo Ferrari and Jody Scheckter at Ferrari's Fiorano test track in 1979 introducing Ferrari's ill-starred 312T5.

Right The Ferraris of pole man Gilles Villeneuve (12) and Jody Scheckter lead Depailler's Ligier (25), Mario Andretti's Lotus (1) and James Hunt's Wolf (20) at the '79 US GP West in Long Beach. Villeneuve won comfortably.

recruited by Ferrari to come up with a decent chassis for 1982, called it the greatest victory he'd ever seen.

Despite his heroics, Villeneuve finished a distant seventh in the championship with Pironi 13th, a lapped fourth in Monaco the Frenchman's best result. But, for the following season, Postlethwaite would come up with a Ferrari worth driving, the 126C2.

Pironi who, to some, was cold, aloof, even arrogant, had gone down well with Enzo Ferrari: "As soon as he arrived he won everyone's admiration and affection, not only for his driving ability but also his way of doing things. He was reserved, while at the same time outgoing," Il Commendatore wrote in his memoirs.

Pironi was also sophisticated, wealthy and well-connected, his house full of art and porcelain. Gilles, by contrast, was very much a petrolhead, happy with his 4x4s and snowmobiles, although now with a penchant for flying helicopters as crazily as he drove cars. Although Villeneuve got on well with Didier from the start, wife Joann was not so sure and warned that Pironi was a political animal.

It was Didier who collaborated with the recently returned Niki Lauda to organize a drivers' strike over new F1 super licence terms ahead of the 1982 season-opener at Kyalami. And Ferrari Motorsport Director Marco Piccinini would be both Pironi's best man at his early 1982 wedding – to which Gilles was not invited – as well as godfather to his children.

But on the track, there was nothing to indicate that Didier was a huge threat to Gilles. A lone point for sixth place in Brazil was all that Ferrari had to show for the first three races of 1982, but the 126C2 was quick, in Villeneuve's hands at any rate. He qualified it third at Kyalami and on the front row in Brazil, Pironi

more than a second adrift both times, but the French-Canadian suffered mechanical problems in the races. He'd also finished third in Long Beach but was disqualified when Tyrrell protested that Ferrari's two-part rear wing was too wide.

The FOCA teams boycotted round four in San Marino after Nelson Piquet and Keke Rosberg were thrown out of first and second places in Brazil following a protest by Ferrari/Renault that their cars had run underweight. Thus, there were just 14 cars at Imola.

The race was clearly going to be between Ferrari and Renault and when the French cars broke down, it was a duel between Villeneuve and Pironi. The Ferraris were marginal on fuel and the team held out the 'slow' board which, Villeneuve interpreted as 'stay in position'. When Pironi passed him to win on the last lap, Gilles was furious, claiming that Didier had stolen it. There was no handshake on the podium and Gilles headed immediately for his helicopter and left.

A couple of days later, Villeneuve spoke to Autosport's Nigel Roebuck, a close friend. "I left because otherwise I'd have said some bad things," Gilles said. "He was looking like the hero who won the race and I looked like the spoilt bastard who sulked. I knew it would look like that, but still thought it was better to get away.

"I haven't said a word to him and I'm not going to again. Ever. I have declared war. I'll do my own thing in future. It's war. Absolutely war.

"Before the race even started we were extremely marginal on fuel. (Mauro) Forghieri told us to save fuel as much as we could. In fact, the cars were topped up on the grid. For three-quarters

Opposite Scheckter joined Ferrari as replacement for departing team leader Carlos Reutemann and was surprised by Villeneuve's raw speed.

Above After Villeneuve won in South Africa and Long Beach early in '79, Scheckter hit back with victories in Belgium and here in Monaco.

Left Villeneuve would honour his commitment to defer to Scheckter in '79, a year that saw the South African win the title.

Opposite Villeneuve and Pironi (smoking) aboard Ferrari's first turbo car, the agricultural 126CK of 1981, which was powerful but unwieldy.

Right Somehow, Villeneuve managed to win with it around the tight confines of Monte Carlo, of all places ...

of the race we were fighting with Arnoux, lapping at around 1minute 35.5seconds. When René blew up I took the lead and we got the 'slow' signal from the pits. I relaxed and slowed the pace. The only thing in my head was making the fuel last. Pironi had dropped back and that let him catch up. I made a mistake coming out of a corner and he passed me.

"I wasn't worried. I figured he'd lead for a couple of laps and then give it back. But what did worry me was that he was going so quickly. I got back in front on lap 49 (of 60) and slowed things down again. Can you imagine two Ferraris leading a race in Italy and running out of fuel on the last lap? I slowed down to 1minute 37 seconds–1 minute 38 seconds for three laps, then he passes me again and we're back in the 1 minute 35 seconds. I thought it was bloody stupid. Then, on lap 59, I passed him again on the approach to Tosa. I thought he lifted a little but he says he had a small engine problem. Whatever it was, I got by and even at that stage I thought he was being honest.

"I went into the last lap so easily you can't believe, still very worried about the fuel. I changed up a thousand revs early. I was almost cruising down the straight before Tosa because I was not expecting him to pass me again. And he comes inside me with wheels almost locked, passes and wins the race. He let me by on lap 59 because he wanted to draft me at the same place on lap 60. And I was stupid enough to believe that he was just being honourable ...

"After the race, I thought that everyone would realize what happened, but no. Pironi says that we both had engine problems, and that there were no team orders, and what really pissed me off was that Piccinini confirmed that to the press. My engine was perfect and there WERE team orders.

"People seem to think we had the battle of our lives! Jesus Christ! I'd been ahead of him most of the race and had qualified a second and a half quicker. Where was my problem? I think I've proved that in equal cars, if I want someone to stay behind me ... Well, I think he stays behind."

A look at the lap times seemed to bear out what Villeneuve claimed. A fortnight later, he had not spoken to Pironi when he went out for his final qualifying run for the Belgian Grand Prix. At the time, F1 cars used super-sticky qualifying tyres that were good for one lap only, so over the course of a qualifying session a driver effectively had two laps on which to set his time. If traffic got in the way, they would often keep their foot in and hope to be seen.

When Villeneuve left the pits on Saturday 8 May at Zolder, there were seven minutes of the session remaining and Pironi was a tenth quicker. At the 150mph left–right beyond the hill after Zolder's back chicane, he caught Jochen Mass's March on a slow-down lap. Villeneuve committed to going for the outside, the racing line out of the left-hander, just as Mass, failing to check his mirrors, moved the same way. The Ferrari was launched into the air, somersaulted and came down nose first in the run-off area sand with such force that the seat belt anchorage points were ripped out. Villeneuve, still attached to his seat, was flung out, landing in the catch fencing on the other side of the track.

Medical officers believed that the initial landing impact was responsible for injuries to Gilles's spinal column, after which he was 'clinically dead'. He was given artificial respiration before

Above Pironi helps return his Ferrari to the pits in practice for the '81 Belgian GP at Zolder.

Right Once he tamed his initial wildness, Villeneuve was widely regarded as F1's fastest man.

Opposite With the Renault of pole man Rene Arnoux invisible, Alain Prost's sister car, the Ferrari 126C2s of Villeneuve and Pironi and Michele Alboreto's Tyrrell prepare for the start of the 1982 San Marino GP. The race caused a rift between Villeneuve and Pironi immediately prior to Gilles's death at Zolder in Belgium less than two weeks later.

being helicoptered to hospital in nearby Louvain, where he officially died shortly after 9pm the same evening. An aircraft of the Canadian Royal Air Force took the body back to Canada, Scheckter accompanying Joann Villeneuve on the flight, for a hero's funeral the following Wednesday. Pironi was informed that he would not be welcome. Didier was in a state of some turmoil. He had survived a huge testing accident at Paul Ricard prior to Brazil, which had actually prompted Villeneuve, in happier days, to quietly tell Roebuck to suggest to the rest of the press contingent that they go easy on Pironi if he was a bit sub-par in Brazil because the shunt had scared the hell out of him.

Then came Imola and Zolder. Pironi was also living a complicated personal life. His 1982 marriage to Catherine Bleynie lasted a matter of weeks. He had fallen in love with actress Veronique Jannot, whom he met at a photo shoot.

But now, the undisputed Ferrari No.1, his ambition to be the first French World Champion was within his grasp. Pironi finished second at Monaco, third in Detroit and then put the Ferrari on pole in Montreal. But he was distraught when he stalled on the grid and, unsighted, 23-year-old Italian rookie Riccardo Paletti, in his second GP, ploughed into the back of the Ferrari. Paletti's Osella caught fire and Pironi bravely grabbed an extinguisher and helped extinguish the flames while F1 medic Sid Watkins worked on Paletti, who sadly succumbed to his injuries.

After Pironi won in Holland, finished second at Brands Hatch and third in France, he led the championship by nine points with five rounds to go. Already on pole with his Friday qualifying time in Germany, with Saturday forecast to be wet all day, Pironi was running flat-out in a wet Saturday morning practice session. Unsighted by spray from Derek Daly's Williams, he pulled out to pass the Williams but failed to spot Alain Prost's Renault in the gloom. In an accident horribly reminiscent of Villeneuve's three months earlier, he was also launched, suffering horrific leg injuries when the car landed and slammed into the barrier. Reigning World Champion Nelson Piquet, first on the scene, tried to get him out of the car but vomited when he saw the state of Pironi's legs.

As Pironi was sedated, he pleaded with Watkins to do everything to save his legs. Skilled surgeons at Heidelberg University hospital managed to achieve that, but Pironi's F1 career was over. His points total was then overhauled by Keke Rosberg, who scraped the title with 44 points from 15 races and a solitary victory at Dijon.

Pironi was not finished with speed. Powerboats were a great passion and in Saint Tropez, near his home, he established his Leader Offshore team. Which is where the author of this book caught up with him in 1986, at which time Pironi was still trying to return to racing despite over 40 operations on his legs.

Speaking of that infamous Imola weekend, he gave his side of the story. "We had a meeting before the race; Arnoux, Prost, Gilles and me, in my motorhome. With so few cars starting we agreed to make a spectacle for the fans for the first half of the race so long as our positions on the lap after half distance were the same as on the grid. We started the real race at half distance and so had plenty of fuel. The team (Ferrari) didn't know that, Marco Piccinini and Gérard Larrousse (Renault's team manager) didn't know. Only the mechanics knew but Prost and Arnoux will tell you the same.

"When I passed Villeneuve the first time, this was because he had made a mistake and gone off the circuit. The first 'slow' sign we got was a few laps after that, and by then we knew we had a lot of fuel left because of the way we'd driven the first half."

That, though, is at odds with Villeneuve, who told Roebuck that at the end of the race his car had enough fuel to do an extra half lap …

With a 40ft carbon fibre/Kevlar Colibri boat, Pironi launched an assault on the 1987 Offshore World Powerboat Championship. Former Ligier teammate Jacques Laffite always said that Pironi, "had massive balls" and, according to racing car constructor Tico Martini, his offshore crewmen started to worry that they were too big.

"They told me they were really frightened," Martini claimed. "He just wouldn't back off, even over big waves. He would argue with his throttle guy, shouting at him 'Don't shut off!'"

Pironi's crew comprised 44-year-old Jean-Claude Guénard, the throttle man, a former motorcycle racer and F3 driver and 37-year-old Bernard Giroux, a former rally co-driver and two-time Paris-Dakar winner. Pironi's ambition was now to win a championship title to make up for the one he had been denied in F1. In mid-August 1987, Didier and his crew took their first victory in Norway. A week later, vying for the lead, they hit the wake of Esso's Avon oil tanker as they reached the turning point in the Needles Trophy race off the Isle of Wight. The craft was launched at 80mph, slammed down upside down, killing all three men.

Pironi, 35 at the time of his death, had been looking forward to becoming a father. His partner, Catherine, was pregnant with twin boys. When they were born, she named them Didier and Gilles. Today, Gilles Pironi works as a reliability engineer with the Mercedes F1 team. Gilles' son Jacques, of course, became World Champion with Williams in 1997, something his father always seemed destined to achieve.

A docufilm telling the tragic stories of Villeneuve and Pironi was due for release in late 2022, with input from both families.

Prost vs. Lauda

Prost
51 Grand Prix wins
4 Championships

Lauda
25 Grand Prix wins
3 Championships

Niki Lauda had made an emotional decision when he walked away from grand prix racing midway through a Montreal Friday practice in 1979. Just over two years later, he asked wife Marlene if she fancied a trip to London to do some shopping at Harrods department store while he attended to some business.

Lauda's 'business' was a secret McLaren test at Donington. There were a couple of factors in play: first, after not remotely missing F1 for a time, he'd now been back in the paddock and realized he missed it. Second, he wanted to expand his airline. Money from racing would certainly help.

But in the two years Niki had been away, speeds had risen, cars ran rock-solid suspension to optimize ground effect aerodynamics and Lauda needed to know if he could still do it. The test at Donington convinced him that he could. Marlene though, was less than impressed. "You're a stupid bastard," she informed him.

McLaren boss Ron Dennis wanted some insurance in case the two-time champion had lost it, so initially they inked a three-month provisional contract. If all went well, it would be a longer deal with a set amount for driving, plus a substantial chunk from Marlboro for Niki's promotional value.

In fact, Lauda won his third race back in 1982, at Long Beach in the USA. He won again at Brands Hatch as he and teammate John Watson, himself a five-time GP winner, proved evenly matched. But after a fatal accident to Gilles Villeneuve and a career-ending one for Ferrari teammate Didier Pironi, it was Keke Rosberg who took the title for Williams with just a single victory.

With turbocharged engines now de rigueur in F1, McLaren was late to the party, commissioning Porsche to develop a V6

turbo financed by team title sponsor Mansour Ojjeh's TAG company. Lauda debuted it midway through the 1983 season at Zandvoort, where it showed great promise. It was a year in which the championship went down to a last round shoot-out between Alain Prost's turbo Renault, the Frenchman leading the series since Belgium in May, and Nelson Piquet's BMW turbo-powered Brabham.

Prost, who had lost out on the title in 1982 by 10 points, was second best to Piquet this time, by just two points, as a turbocharged car won the title for the first time. "One thing's sure, I won't get any closer than that," Prost said.

With Renault now seven years into its F1 turbo programme, the 11th-hour loss was a body blow, the company having flown staff to South Africa to witness its crowning glory. The frustrated Prost criticized a lack of chassis development. A rumoured indiscretion involving team boss Gérard Larrousse's wife probably didn't help, and Alain was fired.

The man regarded as the best in the business – although Piquet might have argued – was quickly snapped up by McLaren's Ron Dennis to partner Lauda in John Barnard's McLaren MP4/2 TAG turbo for 1984. Prost was returning to the team for whom he had driven in 1980 before moving to Renault.

New flat-bottomed F1 regulations in 1983 had given the cars some suspension back and slowed down lap speeds that were getting out of hand, but ever more powerful turbo engines were sending them back north, especially in qualifying trim.

Lauda, a man who started from the pole nine times in both 1974 and 1975, a decade earlier, now found it tough.

"Everything happens so quickly with a turbo in qualifying," he said. "You don't have time to work into a rhythm and suddenly you're presented with 300bhp more. It's like a big kick up the arse and you have to get on with it. I can't handle it as well as some of the others, as simple as that."

The luckless Watson, who'd lost his seat to the unexpectedly available Prost, was not too sure the new McLaren teammates were going to gel. "They're both single-minded, selfish, wanting kind of people," he opined.

In qualifying, certainly, Lauda could not cope with Prost. Barnard recalled, "Niki would say, 'This fucking little Frenchman is always half a second quicker than me and I've got to figure out what to do.' Niki had the nous to suss out his competition and play games with them mentally, but at the end of the day Prost was just quicker. And it used to piss Niki off no end because he couldn't figure out how to find the extra lap time."

A decade later Damon Hill would experience the same phenomenon with Prost at Williams, but at least he could then take away an overlay of their respective laps on Friday and return the next day a little more enlightened.

Now, though, Lauda was 12 years into his F1 life and not prepared to hang it out quite so much as Prost, who still harboured the burning desire to be France's first World Champion.

Over the 16-race 1984 season, Lauda outqualified Prost just once. And while Prost put his McLaren on the front row 10 times, Lauda didn't manage it at all. It got to Lauda and he admitted as much: "I hated the guy. Not personally, but when I saw him I got upset. He was my biggest enemy. And in the same team!"

Prost would come to know those very same feelings four years later, when Ayrton Senna arrived.

One saving grace for Lauda was a new regulation limiting cars to just 220 litres of fuel for the race. In qualifying the turbos could run high-boost qualifying laps – Piquet put the Brabham-BMW on pole nine times with an engine reckoned to be producing 900bhp – but on Sunday afternoons the relatively frugal TAG Porsche V6 turbos gave McLaren a distinct advantage. Porsche, of course, had considerable experience in endurance racing. McLaren would win 12 of the season's 16 races and the championship came down to a straight battle between its two drivers.

Lauda led the season-opening Brazilian GP before retiring and handing victory to Prost. The practice of freezing fuel to get more into the tank had begun and, in South Africa, Prost had to start from the pits in the spare McLaren when a frozen fuel valve knobbled his race car. Lauda won.

Monaco produced the infamous race stoppage that denied Senna a stunning first grand prix win in his debut season with Toleman. Rain, always the great equalizer, had seen Prost leading but an inspired Senna storming through the field. He was catching the lead McLaren at multiple seconds per lap. Prost, knowing the game was up, was pointing to the sky every time he passed the start/finish line, trying to get the race stopped. Clerk of the Course Jacky Ickx waved the red flag at the end of lap 31, Senna having just stormed past the leading McLaren, but the classification was decided at the end of the previous lap, with Prost the winner. Senna actually had damaged suspension through a whack on the

chicane kerbs and, according to Toleman's Pat Symonds, "he may have finished had the race gone on, and he may not …"

With the abandoned race not completing 75% distance, half points were awarded, meaning that instead of nine points, Prost scored 4.5. Had it not been stopped and Alain had finished second to Senna, he would have scored six points. That would become important at season's end. Lauda and Prost finished second and third respectively in Canada, Niki retired in Detroit while Alain finished fourth, and neither finished in a baking hot Dallas GP.

Lauda claimed a third victory at Brands Hatch, where Prost's gearbox broke and so with six races remaining, Alain led Niki by a point and a half in the championship. Prost then won at Hockenheim with Lauda second, but Niki took the championship lead for the first time when he won his home Austrian Grand Prix as Prost spun off on oil.

In Holland, Alain won with Niki second, trimming Niki's championship lead to a single point. Monza though, was crucial, as Lauda scored a fifth victory while Prost suffered an engine failure. With two rounds remaining they had five wins apiece, and Lauda had a 10.5-point lead, meaning that he could afford to finish second to Prost in both remaining races and still win his third world title.

At the penultimate round at a new, shortened Nürburgring some eight years after Lauda's near-fatal, fiery accident in Germany, Prost did indeed win, but a lacklustre race from Lauda saw him qualify 15th, more than 3 seconds slower, and finish fourth.

With Tyrrell disqualified from all 1984 results for the illegal addition of lead ballast to its water tanks, its points were

Opposite **Prost's Renault at Monaco in '81.**

Above **Lauda won the third race of his comeback with McLaren, at Long Beach in '82.**

Right Prost lost out on the 1983
championship with Renault in the final
round at Kyalami.

re-allocated, giving Prost one extra, meaning that heading to the final race of the year in Estoril, Lauda led by 3.5 points. If Alain won, Niki had to be second.

Prost's seventh victory of the year was pretty much a foregone conclusion. Lauda though, made things hard for himself. While Prost started on the front row, Niki qualified 11th, almost a second and a half slower. As so often that season, he had to battle his way through the pack.

"It was the only time I saw Niki just chuck everything at it and go for it big time," said John Barnard, and Keke Rosberg agreed: "Niki drove harder this year than I have ever seen before; absolutely clean and absolutely uncompromising."

By the time Lauda got through into third, he had 37 seconds to make up on Nigel Mansell's second-placed Lotus. The championship hung in the balance.

This was Mansell's last race for Lotus before going to Williams and his relationship with team boss Peter Warr, never strong, had reached rock bottom. Mansell was harder on brakes than teammate Elio de Angelis and Estoril was demanding on brakes. Lotus had just one set of thicker brake pads available, and they went to Elio. With 12 laps remaining Nigel ran out of brakes and spun off. Lauda was second, and champion. If Prost thought he would never get closer than 1983 and lose, he was wrong – he'd lost out by half a point. If only Monaco hadn't been stopped early at his behest …

Lauda reckoned his third championship his greatest achievement but it had taken a lot out of him and he knew he couldn't do it again against Prost. In 1985 Alain did indeed

become the first French World Champion in a season in which he won five times, comfortably heading Ferrari's Michele Alboreto in the championship table. Lauda, with just a lone win in Holland, dropped to 10th after a season in which he had 11 retirements.

"Last year my motivation was to win the championship but this year I have not been able to find a new motivation," he said on announcing his end-of-season retirement at his home race in Austria. "I'm having a bad year, which is nobody's fault, but really I can't find a good reason to go on next year, so I stop."

This time it wasn't emotional, Lauda was really through. He turned his focus and single-mindedness to business. As well as his airline, Lauda became a familiar face in the F1 paddocks as a TV pundit and as a shareholder/director of the Mercedes F1 team. One of F1's greats died in 2019, aged 70, leaving behind a £445 million estate. His funeral held in St Stephens cathedral, Vienna, was attended by a *Who's Who* of motor racing from the last 50 years.

Opposite After losing the '84 championship to McLaren teammate Lauda, Prost took his first world title the following season.

Left Prost prepares for action in Detroit, 1985.

Below Prost leads Jacques Laffite's Williams-Honda at Kyalami in '84.

Piquet vs. Mansell

Piquet
23 Grand Prix wins
3 Championships

Mansell
31 Grand Prix wins
1 Championship

Opposite Nigel Mansell, seen at Paul
Ricard in '81, was given his F1 break
by Lotus founder Colin Chapman.

Right After two World Championships,
Piquet's Brabham career came to a
halt in '85, when he signed with Frank
Williams.

Slim and wiry in physique, Nelson Piquet's stamina could
sometimes be questioned, especially following his 1981 podium
collapse at Caesar's Palace just after he clinched his first world title.
But nobody ever questioned his spirit, speed or car control.

Piquet delighted his fans with a home win in the early season
1982 Brazilian Grand Prix before ... once again collapsing on
the podium. It was not his only sinking feeling that day; shortly
afterwards he and Keke Rosberg were both disqualified for the
'water ballast' ruse that some Cosworth V8-powered teams were
desperately adopting to try to stay competitive with the turbo cars.
They were equipped with water-cooled brakes that took their cars
up to the minimum weight limit, but the water soon disappeared
after the race started, allowing them to compete against the
heavier but far more powerful turbo cars.

By the 1983 season BMW had developed a flat four turbo
which, under the development of Brabham's design genius
Gordon Murray, took Nelson to his second world title; Piquet edging
out Alain Prost and Renault in the very last round in South Africa.

The following two seasons yielded slim pickings as the
McLaren-TAG Porsches dominated the 1984 and 1985 seasons.
In the first of those Piquet's speed was still very much in evidence
as he took nine poles but only managed to win twice, in Montreal
and Detroit, the Brabham-BMW proving too fragile. A surprise switch
to Pirelli tyres in 1985 was a backward step in an era when choosing
the wrong tyre manufacturer could condemn a competitive team
to the sidelines all year.

Now with experience to go with his speed and at the top of
his game, there was no reason not to regard Piquet as the favourite
to win a third world title in six years when, for 1986, he joined the
Williams-Honda team. Bernie Ecclestone was caught on the hop
when Frank Williams did a deal with Piquet in the car park at the
Austrian Grand Prix. Nelson felt that he'd become almost a fixture
at Brabham and that Bernie was offering him less than the going
rate. Ecclestone was notoriously mean as a team boss, reputedly
putting a time switch on the Brabham factory toilets to prevent
his mechanics going in there to read a newspaper. Many felt that
Nelson was the fastest driver in F1, or at least on a par with Prost
and the emerging Senna, so he felt he should be paid as such.

By the end of 1985, the Williams FW10, with its potent Honda V6
turbo, was the class of the F1 field. In his 72nd race Nigel Mansell
took his first win in the European Grand Prix at Brands Hatch and
followed it up with another win in South Africa. Teammate Keke
Rosberg finished off the year with another victory for Williams in
the Australian GP at Adelaide. That was three race wins in a row
for the team, but Keke was on his way to McLaren to partner new
champion Alain Prost, stepping into the race seat vacated by Niki
Lauda who had hung up his helmet for good. The 1986 Williams
line-up would be Nelson and Nigel.

When you consider Mansell's eventual 31 GP win career, it's
easy to forget his perceived status within the F1 community when
Frank signed him in 1984. Born 8 August 1953, in Upton upon Severn,
Worcestershire, he was already 31 and had spent four and a half
seasons at Lotus after Colin Chapman first gave him a third car for
the 1980 Austrian Grand Prix, alongside Mario Andretti and Elio
de Angelis. It was a blessed relief for Nigel when the engine failed
40 laps into the race's 54, a fuel leak into the cockpit having left him

with first and second degree burns to his buttocks. When Andretti moved to Alfa Romeo for 1981, Nigel got the hot seat full time.

The next four seasons saw Lotus in decline, with Chapman dying from a heart attack in 1982 and his successor, Peter Warr, never enjoying any kind of relationship with Mansell. In 1983, at a time when only sponsor, cigarette brand John Player Special was keeping Mansell in a seat, Warr said: "Mansell has been complaining that he has no (turbo) engine. Next year, we'll make sure that he hasn't got a car …" The stats say that over four seasons alongside the late de Angelis (killed in testing at the Paul Ricard circuit) at Lotus, Nigel was outqualified 43–15 by the Italian. Often, though, they weren't in comparable machinery and it was de Angelis who was afforded No.1 treatment.

"We knew we were going to switch out Jacques Laffite for 1985," Frank Williams recalled, "and Ayrton was our original choice but he had signed for Lotus early. I have to confess I was rather dickering around, blowing hot one day and cold the next. Eventually, Patrick (Head, partner and technical director) said, 'For goodness sake, Frank, make a decision and we'll live with it.' So, I went straight out of the motorhome and told Nigel, "Put your signature here …"

There were many in the paddock who thought Frank Williams had made a mistake. "I remember James Hunt making some snide remarks about Mansell but everyone tended to overlook all the positive aspects of his driving. He was exceptionally quick and, on tight circuits, very fast.

"To be honest, though, I thought he would produce what I had expected from Alan Jones in 1978 a good No.2, always in or near the points. No way did I ever think, 'Wow, we've got a potential World Champion.' But, by the second half of 1985, I began to realize that we'd got something a bit special on our hands."

Piquet soon realized it too. After he started 1986 in fabulous style by winning his second Brazilian Grand Prix, while Mansell was taken off in a clash with Senna's Lotus, Nigel drove a great race in Spain to finish second, just 0.014 seconds behind Senna. And now things became tense. Prior to the season, Frank Williams had been involved in a bad car accident returning from a pre-season test at Paul Ricard. For a time, his life hung in the balance and he was left a quadriplegic. He was no longer in control of a team in which Piquet claimed he had No.1 status. Nelson wanted first call on the Williams T-car. In the profligate 1980s, teams could still build up a spare or 'T' (for Training) car. Nelson felt that he'd been guaranteed No.1 status but Frank himself always claimed that was nonsense.

"What Nelson thought he was being guaranteed was a repeat of the Reutemann fiasco of 1981 when we controlled – or tried to control – the second driver," Williams recalled. "What in fact was discussed in the Österreichring car park was that, in a classic case of one driver leading the championship and needing every bit of support, then we would obviously control his teammate. But he was not given unconditional priority. We took the view that they were both fighting for the championship and would have to fight it out between them."

Piquet's nose was put further out of joint when Patrick Head himself took over the engineering responsibility on Mansell's car. It happened because Sergio Rinland, who had engineered Nigel at the start of the year, left the team, and Patrick filled the gap.

Opposite Mansell's JPS Lotus in the pits at the '83 Austrian GP at Österreichring.

Above Mansell's Williams-Honda disputes the first corner of the 1985 European GP with Ayrton Senna. The race gave Nigel his first GP win at the 72nd attempt.

Left Nigel, 'the People's Champion', tests at Estoril in early '86.

Right Mansell won a great fight with Williams teammate Piquet in the 1986 British GP at Brands Hatch, in Nelson's spare car ...

"Nelson took this very seriously," Frank explained. "He felt he was being short-changed. Maybe, with hindsight, we should have taken Frank Dernie off Nelson's car and switched them around.

"In fairness to Nelson, while he diligently came to see me in hospital after every race, he never complained about it until I was back at work. Then he came to the factory in August and I remember him sitting there, eyes moist, saying he was desperately concerned, feeling that he was not getting a fair crack of the whip, that Nigel was getting preferential treatment. I tried very hard to disabuse him of that notion."

On the track, it was going Mansell's way. Piquet despised Monaco and it was he that delivered the famous quote, that 'driving at Monaco was like trying to ride a bike in your living room' – and while Nigel put his car on the front row, Nelson qualified 11th, more than 2.2 seconds slower. Mansell finished fourth; Nelson out of the points. When Mansell then won the next two races in Belgium and Canada he moved to within two points of Alain Prost's championship lead and eight points clear of Nelson.

After a fifth place in Detroit, Nigel took back-to-back wins in France and at Brands Hatch where, in Nelson's spare car after a restart, he drove a sensational race to overhaul pole man Piquet and take his second successive hugely popular win. He now led the championship by four points and was 18 points – two victories – clear of his teammate. Nigel had now won six of the previous 12 grands prix. Not bad, as Mark Webber would famously tell Christian Horner in 2010, for a No.2.

Piquet hit back at Hockenheim, where Mansell was third, with the same result also happening at the inaugural Hungarian

GP. Nelson's victory included a superb first corner outside pass of Senna's Lotus. No mean feat – Brazilian passing Brazilian.

Now it was Nigel's turn to feel disgruntled, feeling that Piquet had duped him over the benefits of a new 'trick' differential that the Brazilian had raced. Frank Dernie always denied that, however, saying that Mansell had tried it in practice and discarded it in favour of the standard one.

When they were fourth and fifth respectively in Mexico, it meant that Mansell would go into the season-closing Australian GP in Adelaide with 70 points to Alain Prost's 64 and Piquet's 63. A third place would wrap it up for Nigel.

Goodyear's pre-race information was that a non-stop run would not be possible, so both Mansell and Piquet planned tyre stops. However, when Prost suffered a puncture while lapping Gerhard Berger on lap 32 of the race's 82, tyre technicians assessed the state of his used rubber and revised their opinion on the possibility of completing the race without a stop. This information reached Williams and they maintained a watching brief.

However, on lap 62, race leader Keke Rosberg, in his last grand prix, suffered a McLaren tyre failure. Piquet and Mansell had been running 2 and 3, Nigel on course for the title when, a lap later, he too suffered a spectacular left rear tyre blow-out, producing iconic images as he wrestled the car to a standstill in the Adelaide escape road, gut-wrenchingly close to his life's ambition.

Feeling it irresponsible to take any risks with Piquet, Nelson was called in, which promoted Prost to the lead and allowed him to steal a second championship title from under the noses of the Williams men. Called into the London BBC TV studios to watch the race in

Right When Piquet went from Williams to Lotus-Honda for '88, replacing Senna, Frank lost his engines to Ayrton's new team, McLaren.

Below The grid for the '87 French GP at Paul Ricard with Mansell's Williams on pole, from Prost's McLaren, Senna's Lotus and Piquet.

Opposite Mansell took pole and led convincingly before retiring with a turbo failure at Monaco in '87.

the early hours of the morning with wife Ginny, Frank Williams was left sadly shaking his head. The Williams drivers had won nine of 16 races, but not the title. Williams, though, had beaten McLaren to the constructors' title by 149 points to 96. Over the 1986 season Mansell won five races to Piquet's four and they were 8–8 in qualifying. Mansell's reputation was hugely enhanced, Piquet's diminished.

The following season, it was more of the same. Mansell undeniably had more pace as the Williams-Honda FW11B was even more dominant than the previous year's car, but four retirements and a crash at Suzuka, which saw him miss the final two rounds, handed a third world title to Piquet, who achieved the feat with just three race victories to Nigel's six. Five second places in the first seven races and then three mid-season victories in four races were the bedrock for the more canny Nelson, who drove for points above wins.

It was actually a brave effort from the Brazilian, who suffered an enormous crash at Imola's notorious Tamburello curve when a tyre deflated in practice. He was forced to miss the San Marino Grand Prix, only the second race of the season, with concussion, after which he had sleep problems and balance issues for longer than he cared to admit.

The intra-team atmosphere between the drivers had become toxic and, by August, Piquet had done a deal to join Lotus-Honda for 1988, replacing Senna. Ayrton was on his way to McLaren, which had taken Williams' all-important Honda engine supply. Piquet's freely given criticism that Williams had lost the championship to Prost in 1986 because it lacked leadership with Frank away, and failed to control Mansell, had not helped

the team's ability to retain Honda engines. They were left to struggle with a Judd V10 for the following season.

Over the two seasons together, Mansell won 11 races to Piquet's seven and outqualified him 17–12. Not bad for a 'mid-grid driver' against a three-times World Champion. Doubtless that stuck in Nelson's psyche and, at the start of the following year, in an interview with *Brazilian Playboy,* he labelled Mansell an "uneducated blockhead" and, called his wife, Rosanne, "ugly". Given their respective builds and strength it was either brave, stupid or both. Piquet's penchant for unsavoury and offensive statements continued during and following his driving career. He publicly questioned Ayrton Senna's sexuality and called him the "São Paulo taxi driver", described Enzo Ferrari as "senile" and used the racially pejorative Portuguese term "negulnho" when referring to Lewis Hamilton. Despite an apology, the latter subsequently resulted in Piquet being banned from the F1 paddock for life as of July 2022.

Senna vs. Prost

Senna
41 Grand Prix wins
3 Championships

Prost
51 Grand Prix wins
4 Championships

Alain 'The Professor' Prost could have won four successive world titles between 1983 and 1986, but the way the cards fell he had to be content with just two for McLaren. Piquet edged past him in 1983, and his teammate Niki Lauda beat him by half a point in 1984, the slimmest of margins barring a tied score and the countback of first and second places.

But the man who would truly engage all his driving and political combativity was just emerging on the scene. Born 1 March 1960, to a wealthy family in São Paulo, Brazil, Ayrton Senna had come in to Formula 1 after duking it out with Martin Brundle in British F3, a time when the future Sky commentator was run by a fledgling Eddie Jordan team and pushing Senna to the absolute limit.

Had Ayrton come into F1 with the best team – McLaren in 1984 – there's little doubt that he could have challenged for the championship in his first season of F1, just as Lewis Hamilton did with McLaren 23 years later. Senna, though, had to wait. The Toleman-Hart he made his debut with was not a front-running team, unless it was Monaco and wet, when Senna's skill behind the wheel was the great equalizer.

Joining Lotus for 1985, Ayrton immediately proved he had amazing single lap skill. The Renault turbo engines were potent enough for him to start from pole in his second race at Estoril and when it rained on race day, there was no one touching the Lotus 97T. But, in the dry, the Renault was not as fuel-efficient as the Hondas, in particular, meaning reduced boost and a tough job come race day on Sunday. He qualified on pole at the following race the San Marino Grand Prix at Imola, but ran out of fuel and was classified seventh.

There were eight poles and two more wins at Jerez and Detroit in 1986, Senna hoping that a switch to Honda engines for 1987 would see Lotus compete with Williams, who had dominated the two previous seasons with the same engine. It didn't happen; the Lotus 99T was far from the best chassis to come out of the team's Hethel, Norfolk base, although Senna's precision on tight street circuits, where power was not the deciding factor, saw it first past the chequered flag in Monaco and Detroit again.

Ayrton was frustrated at four seasons of being unable to launch a championship assault, but that was about to change. For 1988 he joined McLaren, which had prised the Honda engine supply away from Frank Williams, citing that the Didcot team had been unable to manage the friction between their two leading drivers …

Alain was 33 and facing perhaps the fastest man ever to drive a grand prix car, who now had four years' F1 experience and 16 pole positions. Keke Rosberg, who had been stunned by Prost's pace when the Finn replaced Niki Lauda at McLaren, thought that alongside Alain, Ayrton would be nobody. But Keke had that badly wrong …

Upping the ante, McLaren's new MP4/4 would become one of the greatest F1 cars of all time. When it turned up late at a pre-season Imola test, within half an hour it was two seconds quicker than any other car over the previous three days. McLaren boss Ron Dennis told his staff that they could win every race.

The McLaren team co-ordinator was Mexican Jo Ramírez, who had a ringside view of the two teammates/combatants: "From the very first time Ayrton drove the MP4/4, he had an obsession about Alain. He wanted to know what rear wing he had, which

front springs, which tyres. Every time he came into the pits the first thing he'd ask was what time Alain had done.

"Alain used to laugh, but he soon realized what a threat Ayrton was. It was at Imola, at the end of qualifying for round two. Alain always used to get back to the truck and change quickly. Ayrton was a bit more methodical. When he changed, he'd fold things up and put them away. Then he'd always sit in the truck and kind of meditate. Alain had finished changing and just as he was walking out, he stopped where I was standing, looking at the times.

"Alain was resting on the cabinet with his back to Ayrton, who was sitting on the floor a bit further up the truck. Ayrton was a lot quicker and Alain just didn't understand how he was so fast. He looked at the split times and then half-turned to me and whispered, 'Shit, he's quick!'

"But Ayrton heard it. And he just looked up at me and winked. At that moment I thought to myself, okay Ayrton, you're halfway there …"

Senna had already outqualified Prost by seven-tenths at the first race in his native Brazil but when the car was stuck in first gear on the grid and the start aborted, Ayrton was forced into the T-car and later disqualified as the race had been merely delayed rather than restarted. So, Prost won Senna's home grand prix, much to the Brazilian's dismay.

At Imola, Senna hit back and then, in qualifying at Monaco, drove a totally surreal pole lap. "I was way over the limit but still trying to find even more," Senna said. "Then, suddenly, something kicked me. I kind of woke up and realized that I was in a different atmosphere than normal. I drove back to the pits slowly and didn't

want to go out any more that day. It frightened me because I realized that I was way beyond my conscious understanding."

There were those who believed that Senna didn't just want to beat Prost, but humiliate him. His pole was a second and a half quicker than Alain's second place time and 2.6 seconds clear of anyone else. But then, leading the race by almost a minute with 12 laps to go, Senna had a lapse of concentration and hit the barrier at Portier. Distraught, he went straight back to his Monaco apartment and was incommunicado for the rest of the day.

Prost inherited the win and when he was victorious in Mexico as well, he was 18 points clear of Senna in the championship. Such was the McLaren superiority that every time Prost finished, he was either first or second. And he only failed to finish twice. It was going to be a tough gap for Senna to close, notwithstanding that only the best 11 of a driver's 16 races would count (the practice of counting every round only began in 1991).

Senna won in Canada and Detroit with Prost second, the order reversed in France before the F1 circus headed for Silverstone. This was the race that Senna got himself back in the championship fight, making a nine-point gain as Prost simply gave up in the pouring rain. Alain was taken to task by sections of the media for this, but his decision had its roots in events at Hockenheim six years earlier when Didier Pironi, unsighted by spray, was horribly injured when his Ferrari took off over the back of Prost's Renault in a career-ending accident.

"I think motor racing should be run in the dry," he said at the time. "Look at the Open golf – they cancelled the third day because the weather was so bad and the worst that was going

Opposite Senna and Prost before things turned sour, celebrating a 1-2 in the '88 season-closing Australian GP in Adelaide.

Left Senna took the first of his three world titles with McLaren in '88.

Below The decisive moment of the '89 World Championship in Japan. Prost is already out of his car after a slow-speed crash with Senna which clinched him the championship. Ayrton re-started, won the race, but was subsequently excluded in a travesty of a decision by stewards of the FIA under French president Jean-Marie Balestre.

Right Imola '89, the race that killed relations between Senna (seen leading the first start) and Prost, with Alain accusing Ayrton of breaking an agreement when the race was restarted following an accident to Gerhard Berger.

Above A dejected Senna contemplates life after retiring from the 1990 Spanish GP at Jerez with engine problems.

Right Senna and Prost head back to the pits after Ayrton took out Alain at the first corner of the 1990 Japanese GP at Suzuka, to clinch his second World Championship. 'An eye for an eye after last year,' was the way Senna viewed it.

Opposite Nigel Mansell and Prost, pictured with test driver Gianni Morbidelli, were Ferrari teammates in 1990.

to happen was that the players would get wet. They don't race IndyCars in the wet either. It's my life and my judgement."

Senna's win brought him to within six points of Prost and when Ayrton won at Hockenheim and the Hungaroring ahead of Alain, the two drivers were level on 66 points. A fourth straight win, at Spa, put Senna in front for the first time and he clinched the title with a fantastic win at Suzuka after stalling in pole position. Normally that would have meant a humiliating exit from the race, but because the Suzuka start/finish straight slopes downhill towards Turn 1, Ayrton was able to bump start the McLaren and recover, though he had dropped to 14th place. On the opening lap he passed six cars, shades of what was to come in Donington 1993, one of the best ever opening laps in a grand prix.

"Until today I always said my best drive was Estoril in 1985, my first win, but not anymore. This was the best," Senna said. McLaren had not quite managed to match Dennis's pre-season prediction: Senna and Prost had won 15 of the 16 races, the clean sweep denied by Senna being punted out by backmarker Jean-Louis Schlesser's Williams at Monza.

In 1989, the relationship between Senna and Prost fell apart. It started at Imola, where the McLaren drivers had an agreement that whoever made the better start would lead into the Tosa left-hander further around the lap. First time up, that was Senna. The race though, was stopped when Gerhard Berger's Ferrari crashed and burst into flames in an accident not unlike Romain Grosjean's in Bahrain 30 years later.

For the next start, Prost made the better getaway but Senna was quicker out of the flat-out Tamburello and was already alongside and marginally ahead rounding Villeneuve, the corner before Tosa. Whether or not Senna had contravened the agreement depended on the precise interpretation of the word 'start'. Did it include just Tamburello or also the run down the following straight?

Prost kicked up a huge fuss about it, claiming he was robbed, which was a little disingenuous considering he'd finished some 40 seconds behind … It was hardly an Imola spat of Villeneuve/Pironi proportions but the media ramped it up and Ron Dennis felt obliged to visit a pre-Monaco test at Pembrey in Wales the following week to try to calm things down.

The performance pattern in 1989 was much the same as in 1988 with Senna starting from pole 13 times and Prost just twice. But, after a hat-trick of victories in San Marino, Monaco and Mexico, Senna had an appalling run of misfortune. There was an electrical problem in Phoenix, engine failure in Canada, a transmission issue in France, a gearbox problem at Silverstone, another blown engine in Monza, a collision with Mansell (who shouldn't have been on the track after being black-flagged) in Portugal.

Whenever Senna finished he invariably won, which happened six times. But such was the unreliability that he could only muster an additional second place to go towards his 11 best scores. Prost, meanwhile, had four wins, six seconds and a third. Heading to the penultimate round in Japan, Prost could only add to his score by winning or finishing second. Senna would overhaul him if he won the final two races, which looked a real possibility.

Prost prioritized race set-up in Japan and had a Gurney flap on his car removed for greater straightline speed. He managed to

beat pole man Senna away from the line and, going hard, opened a 6 second lead. But, after tyre stops and a set-up change in the pits, Senna was back on his tail by lap 40. Prost, by now, had fallen out with McLaren. He had already signed with Ferrari for 1990 and, after winning at Monza, had deeply offended Ron Dennis by giving the Italian GP trophy away. Dennis liked to keep his trophies, suitably polished, nicely in order, in a display cabinet in the reception at McLaren's Woking base.

Prior to the race, Prost pointed out that in previous instances when they had been racing wheel to wheel, he would leave the door open for Senna, but on this occasion he would not. Sure enough, as Senna made a better exit from the high-speed 130R corner and made a bid for the inside of Suzuka's final chicane, Prost moved over on him. Contact was made and both cars came to a halt with stalled engines. Alain hopped out, convinced the title was his. Senna, however, signalled marshals to push him down the escape road, managed to bump start his engine, pitted for a new nose, rejoined, passed new leader Alessandro Nannini, and won the race.

Stewards, however, disqualified him for missing out the chicane. Some suggest this might have been under the direction of then FISA president, Frenchman Jean-Marie Balestre. Whatever the case, it was travesty of a decision. Prost had caused the accident. The rules say that in such a situation, cars should be pushed into a safe position, which is why Senna steered down the escape road. When he put his case, Ayrton was asked why he hadn't turned around and completed the chicane. He answered that doing that would have broken a rule saying that you cannot

Right Senna at Phoenix in '91, the year of his third title in four seasons with McLaren.

Below Prost took a fourth World Championship at Williams in '93 before hanging up his helmet.

Opposite Senna was delighted to get the better of Prost in the final two races of '93, the last times they competed against each other, after a dominant season for the Frenchman at Williams.

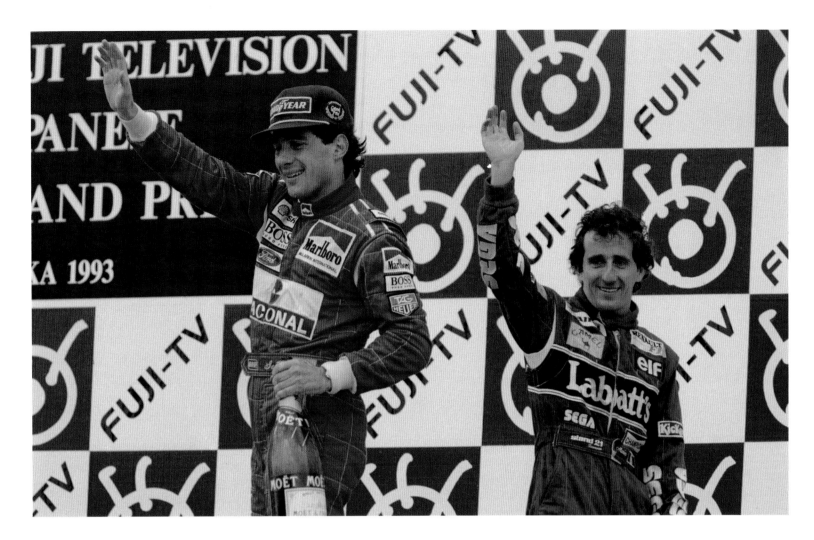

drive in an opposing direction to race traffic, something Mike Hawthorn had been accused of back in the 1950s.

McLaren appealed and Dennis even flew back from Japan to the Heathrow Penta hotel to brief a press room of journalists about the case before heading back out to the Adelaide season finale. Among the evidence submitted was helicopter footage revealing Prost turning in early and initiating the contact, plus several instances showing drivers having an issue and rejoining after missing a part of the circuit, without penalty. The ultimate irony was that Prost had done just that at the controversial Imola race the same year on the way to his six points!

It looked as if the appeal decision against Senna was decided before the court even convened, FISA suddenly presenting irrelevant spurious accusations relating to earlier races and labelling the Brazilian 'a dangerous driver.' Not only was the appeal denied, but Senna was fined $100,000 and given a six-month suspended ban.

"Last year at the Seoul Olympics, I watched the boxer, Roy Jones Junior in the Light Middleweight final," said a leading sports journalist. "He won every round and landed 86 punches to Korean opponent Park-Si Hun's 32. He was also awarded the outstanding boxer of the games accolade. But the administrators were Korean and they gave the decision and the gold medal to their own man. It was the worst decision I've seen in sport. This smells just as bad ..."

The intra-team McLaren rivalry has been written about in great depth. But looking at the data, was it really that close? Senna won 14 of the 32 races (15 if you include the Suzuka stitch-up) to

Alain's 11, but without the unreliability that owed nothing to Ayrton, it would have been more like 18–8. Senna took 26 pole positions to Prost's four, outqualified him 28–4, with an average qualifying gap between them of 0.67 seconds. It was hardly Hamilton versus Verstappen.

The following year, with Prost now at Ferrari, he and Senna fought out the championship for the third successive year. Once again it ended in acrimony in Japan, where this time it was Prost who needed to finish the race. Senna believed that pole ought to be changed to the conventional place for P1, the grippy racing line on the outside and was told it would be, until Balestre ruled otherwise. When Prost made the better getaway from P2 on that grippier part of the track, Senna had no compunction about barging down his inside at Turn 1 and punting him off. As far as Ayrton was concerned, looking back at the collision and politicking of 1989, it was an eye for an eye. Senna was World Champion and, in 1991, won the title for a third time. Prost, after unadvisedly calling his Ferrari a "truck" at the 1991 Japanese Grand Prix was fired once more and spent 1992 on a sabbatical.

In 1993 he returned to replace Nigel Mansell in the dominant Williams team and cantered to a fourth world title alongside trouble-free teammate Damon Hill. But Frank Williams had already signed Senna for 1994 and, rather than rejoin battle against Senna once more in the same car, Alain hung up his helmet. Relations between the two drivers had only just started to thaw when Senna was killed at the San Marino Grand Prix, ending the chance of a future rapprochement.

Hill vs. Schumacher

Hill
22 Grand Prix wins
1 Championship

Schumacher
91 Grand Prix wins
7 Championships

The 1994 Formula 1 season was turbulent, tragic, controversial and utterly compelling. It began with Ayrton Senna, the greatest driver of his generation, possibly of all time, newly installed at Williams, the dominant team of the day. Between 1992 and 1997 Williams won the F1 Constructors' Championship five times out of six.

Williams had stolen a march on its rivals with its active ride FW14B car that had taken Nigel Mansell to a comfortable 1992 World Championship, with Alain Prost following up in 1993 in the FW15, a car in which he won seven times. That same year also witnessed a mid-season hat-trick of victories for teammate Damon Hill.

Frank Williams, though, had already signed Senna for 1994 as Hill's replacement. When Prost realized what was on the cards, he decided to retire rather than face another season in the same car as Senna. He would put his energies towards creating his own F1 team.

On the surface, F1's commercial supremo Bernie Ecclestone had a dilemma: how was he going to promote a championship with the best driver in the best team and the outcome a foregone conclusion …?

Although it wasn't quite that simple. At the end of the 1993 season, the FIA had banned many of the electronic driver aids that had become a feature of the most advanced F1 cars ever to arrive on the grid and which, Senna believed, removed fundamental skills intrinsic to driving and competing. Ironically Senna, who had been hugely frustrated by the Williams domination of the previous two seasons while at McLaren, had joined the team just as it lost its key advantages.

Over at Benetton, Michael Schumacher was an emerging force. After a sensational debut with Jordan in 1991, standing in for the jailed Bertrand Gachot, Michael had been poached by the Flavio Briatore-run team. He scored his debut victory at Spa in 1992. In 1993 he finished fourth in the Drivers' Championship behind the Williams drivers and Senna. Whenever he finished a race in 1993 it was on the podium. Benetton team principal Tom Walkinshaw, asked whether he was going to try and talk Alain Prost out of retirement for 1994, responded, "Why would I? I've got Schumacher …"

In pre-season testing it became clear that Benetton's B194 with Schumacher at the wheel was going to be a threat. Senna, Hill and Williams were slower than anticipated. In his book *How to Design a Car*, technical guru Adrian Newey admits that Williams had been hurt more than expected by the change back from active to passive suspension and, in retrospect, should have done more to develop a car better aerodynamically suited to a larger range of ride heights.

When Hill tested at the bumpy Nogaro circuit in France he experienced aerodynamic stall so bad that the car jumped around to the extent that he could barely see. After Senna failed to win either of the first two races, at home in São Paulo and at Aida in Japan, he crashed fatally in the San Marino Grand Prix.

It sent a seismic shock through motor racing in much the same way that the death of Jim Clark – the star of his era – in a Formula 2 race at Hockenheim had done in 1968. And there was a slightly eerie similarity to the scenario as far as Hill was concerned, as Clark had been widely predicted to win the title that year.

Back in 1968 the Lotus F1 line-up was Clark and Graham Hill, father of Damon and the 1962 World Champion with BRM. Lotus founder Colin Chapman had been incredibly close to Clark and after Jim's death momentarily considered giving it all up. But Hill stepped up, rallied the devastated team, won the next two grands prix in Spain and Monaco and went on to clinch a second world title in the season finale.

Seven years later Graham Hill, who had retired from driving to manage his own F1 team, died on 29 November when he crashed his Piper Aztec light aircraft on the approach to Elstree aerodrome. He was returning from a team test at Paul Ricard.
The accident also claimed the lives of talented young British driver Tony Brise, team manager Ray Brimble and two mechanics.

Damon, born on 17 September 1960, like his father, was a relative latecomer to motor racing, having previously enjoyed motorbike racing success before embarking on his first full season on four wheels in Formula Ford in 1985 at the age of 24. He proved to be a race winner in all the junior categories he contested but did not make his F1 debut until 1992, in a woeful car for the fast-fading Brabham team. In the days of unlimited testing his big opportunity came as test driver for Williams when he accumulated many thousands of miles in F1's best car as the Didcot-based team developed its active ride car.

When Nigel Mansell won the title with it in 1992 he was unaware that Frank Williams had already signed Prost for 1993. Nigel jumped ship to the IndyCar series when Williams refused to pay what Mansell thought was due to him as the new World Champion. There followed internal debate as to whether Hill

should be promoted to the race team alongside Prost. He had impressed with his testing feedback but before inking a contract, Williams wanted just one more late-season test … at Paul Ricard.

Hill recalls it as somewhat traumatic. "I was living in Clapham, it was the inaugural season of the Premier League with matches played on a Sunday, which caught me out. Chelsea had been at home to Leeds and the traffic in West London was gridlocked. I ended up driving like a maniac to catch my flight to the south of France. They'd have been less than impressed if I'd not shown up.

"I made the plane … just … and slumped down in my seat. I'd almost recovered my composure when I looked down at my watch and realized that it was 29 November, and the identical hour that my father had been in the air on that awful night 17 years before, flying back from Ricard. I felt very uneasy for the remainder of the flight. After that, driving the Williams was the easy part!"

Hill got the gig of course, but now, just 18 months later, had to step into the team leader's role and attempt to raise the spirits of the shattered Williams team. Just as his father had done at Lotus in May 1968, Damon rallied the team with victory in the Spanish GP, where he beat pole man Schumacher who had to settle for second place, Michael stuck in fifth gear for most of the afternoon.

As far as the championship was concerned, though, it seemed like an insurmountable task. Schumacher had won four of the opening five rounds in the 16-race season and finished second in the other. And so, under the 10-6-4-3-2-1-point scoring system for the top six finishers, Michael already had 46 points; Damon, just 16.

Since the start of the season there had been strong political mutterings about the legality of the car built in Enstone. Such had

Opposite Michael Schumacher announced himself to the international motorsport world via his performances in a Mercedes sportscar in '91, racing against Tom Walkinshaw-run Jaguars. The Scot was also active in F1 with Benetton, who would swoop for Schumacher later that year.

Left Hill in an uncompetitive Brabham at Silverstone in '92 before earning his chance with Williams.

Below Schumacher was given his first F1 test by Jordan at Silverstone.

Above Schumacher took his first GP victory in the '92 Belgian GP at Spa.

Right Michael also made his F1 debut at Spa, with Jordan in '91.

Opposite Hill, now a Williams driver alongside Prost, spins out at Imola in '93. He went on to score a hat-trick of wins that year.

been the pace of the Benetton in Schumacher's hands – especially the rocket starts – that prior to his death, Senna had been convinced that Benetton was still using banned driver aids, such as launch and traction control. Having ended his first two races early he had had time to listen and observe Schumacher's car. After the tragic Imola race, the FIA had taken the electronic control boxes from several cars, including the Benetton, for further analysis by its independent specialists, LDRA (Liverpool Data Research Associates).

As an aside, Ford, suppliers of Benetton's HB V8 engines, was running an advert in the motorsport press at the time, featuring a helmeted Schumacher holding an electronic control unit. Mimicking the famed Black Magic chocolates slogan, it said, "Who knows the secret of the black magic box?" After the announcement of the investigation, the advert was rapidly pulled.

Meanwhile, FIA president Max Mosley's reaction to the Senna accident was to make a number of immediate changes to the cars and circuits for safety reasons, which meant that they had to be done straight away rather than 18 months further down the road. This antagonized team principals, Benetton's Flavio Briatore in particular, who declared Mosley and the FIA unfit to be running the sport. Probably not the smartest move in the circumstances given the power that Max wielded.

After Schumacher also won in Canada and France with Hill second, the wheels started to fall off Benetton's season. At Silverstone, Hill had taken pole by 0.003 seconds and, on both formation laps – the second after Martin Brundle's engine had blown – Schumacher briefly overtook him, an illegal move that

smacked of gamesmanship (something that Max Verstappen has also got into trouble for).

Benetton claimed that Williams, aware of cooling limitations with Michael's engine, had instructed Hill to go particularly slowly and Schumacher was only making sure he got a blast of cold air through the radiators. Whatever, on lap 14, Schumacher was given a 5 second stop-go penalty for the offence.

Its notification, however, had not been served within the required time, and Schumacher was told to keep going while the team argued about it. When Michael failed to stop, he was twice shown the black flag, which he ignored, later claiming he hadn't seen it. The black flag was withdrawn and Schumacher finally served his penalty 27 laps into the race's 60. He went on to finish second to a delighted Hill, who enjoyed one of his proudest moments winning his home grand prix, a feat his father never managed, and received the trophy from Princess Diana.

There was a degree of smugness at Benetton when they escaped a post-race stewards' investigation with a $25,000 team fine and a reprimand for Schumacher. It was short-lived, however. Mosley was far from satisfied with that and, a few days later, summoned Benetton before the World Motor Sport Council. Ignoring a black flag was viewed as a serious crime and there had been precedent in the 1989 Portuguese GP when Mansell had received a one-race ban for the same offence. Schumacher's claim that he had not seen the flag was seen as a lie, viewed as unacceptable and he was disqualified from his Silverstone second place and given a two-race ban. And Benetton's fine was upped to $500,000. All rooted in momentarily overtaking

Right One of the most memorable moments of Damon Hill's career, winning the British GP, a feat his father never managed, with Williams in '94 in the presence of HRH Princess Diana.

HITACHI
HITACHI
HITACHI
HITACHI
HITACHI
BRITIS
GRAND
SILVER
Racing
elf
Racing

on the formation lap. Briatore may well have reflected on those accusations of incompetence levelled at the FIA president …

Next on the calendar was Hockenheim with its flat-out straights, ironically the venue for Schumacher's home race but likely to be one of the weakest tracks for Benetton with its V8 Ford engines, versus the more powerful Renault V10s powering Williams. Briatore, therefore, was resolved to miss it. However, the German Grand Prix without Schumacher, the nation's great motor racing hero, would have been a major setback for the Hockenheim promoters. The team thought long and hard over whether to race in Germany on such an unfavourable circuit, or to lodge an appeal and delay the ban; in the event they opted for the latter so as not to disappoint the fans. Schumacher therefore raced at home. In the event neither scored, Schumacher suffering a blown engine and Hill – who had started to receive death threats from German fans – missing a golden opportunity when an attempt to overtake Ukyo Katayama's Tyrrell went awry.

Schumacher then beat Hill at the Hungaroring and Spa before being disqualified from his Belgian win when a new underbody plank that had been introduced in Germany to raise ride heights and further slow down cars, was found to be thinner than the statutory 10mm. Hill inherited the win. When Michael's two-race ban was upheld at appeal and Damon won both races that he missed in Monza and Estoril, it put a very different complexion on the championship. Schumacher now led by 76 points to 75 with three races remaining.

It was now that the mind games started. While Schumacher was building a reputation for ruthlessness on the circuit, he was not usually disrespectful off it, so a vitriolic attack on Hill in the media before the European GP at Jerez was out of character. Michael got stuck in, saying that Hill was not a world-class driver and implying that Nigel Mansell (who had returned from IndyCar to drive the French GP mid-season and would drive the final three races) and rookie David Coulthard were quicker.

"It's interesting to see the performance of Coulthard, who has shown himself to be very quick and had to move over for Hill at both Monza and Estoril," he pointed out. "I've learned nothing about Damon's weaknesses because he's never been under any pressure. I have already known his weak points for some time … I think it's great for me that Mansell is coming to take the place of Coulthard because that's going to put Hill under great pressure."

Damon refused to take the bait: "He's clutching at straws, really. I think I've already answered these questions a hundred times. I have plenty of respect for Michael, I'd be pretty ignorant not to, but I have always worked on the premise that nobody is unbeatable. My dad beat Jim Clark. Examples like that remind you that everyone puts their trousers on one leg at a time."

Maybe Schumacher was reacting to all the politicking that had characterized the year. The result of the post-Imola investigations on the car's electronic control unit was that the Benetton did have software capable of breaching the rules with regards to the use of banned launch/traction control, but the governing FIA had no evidence that it had been used.

The teams' defence, proffered by technical director Ross Brawn, was that it was much easier to disable software that had been allowable before the driver aids ban than to write all-new code.

Opposite Ayrton Senna and Schumacher lead the field away at the start of the tragic San Marino GP of '94, the race that claimed Senna's life.

Above One for the cameras. Schumacher and Hill shake hands after Michael uncharacteristically trash-talked Damon during the '94 championship run-in.

Left Oops ... Schumacher overdoes it looking for those last few hundredths in practice for the '94 Adelaide season finale.

Schumacher's electrifying start at the French Grand Prix, when he blasted past the Williams front row of Hill and Mansell with his less powerful Ford HB, had further fanned the flames. "We've done a lot of development on a new clutch," Schumacher smiled later, while Brawn offered that it was down to Michael's opportunism. Pitlane cynics pointed out that given the massive Research and Development programme F1 teams ran, writing a new bit of software code for the car was not a big ask. And what exactly was the role of the engineer with a laptop at the side of the car on the grid, lingering there moments before the race started …?

In Schumacher's mind, the FIA had contrived a championship showdown by effectively removing him from a quarter of the season with the Silverstone/Spa disqualifications and his two-race ban. But by now, Hill's Williams was a very different proposition from the bucking beast that had started the year. Adrian Newey had identified aerodynamic stall caused by the car's longer sidepods and a shorter podded upgrade had addressed the issue. The end-of-season Williams was much more competitive.

Schumacher comfortably beat Hill to win the European GP in Portugal, while three weeks later Damon hit back with one of his best-ever drives to edge Michael in an aggregated result after a race stoppage at a wet Suzuka. Schumacher therefore took his single-point advantage, 92 points to 91, to the season finale in Adelaide a week later. That slender margin meant, of course, that Michael could afford a race-ending contact but Damon could not.

It was something the FIA did not want to contemplate. The integrity of Formula 1 had been undermined by Ayrton Senna's confession in 1991 that he had deliberately driven into Alain Prost at

Suzuka to win the World Championship, the Brazilian being ahead on points at the time. And Michael had 'previous'. Back in his Formula 3 days he was contending with Mika Häkkinen to win the prestigious Macau GP, in a race won on aggregate times. Häkkinen only had to follow him home to win the race, but decided to go for a gap Schumi had left and was walloped by the German driver.

Mansell pipped Schumacher to the Australian pole by two-hundredths, Michael trying so hard that he shunted the Benetton. Damon initially seemed out of sorts, almost seven-tenths down, his mood not improved by Williams contract negotiations that he felt did not reflect the worth of a now nine-time GP winner.

Despite his pole, Mansell said he would not interfere with the championship battle and was more intent on protecting Williams' five-point advantage over Benetton in the Constructors' Championship. As good as his word, he did not fight too hard as Schumacher and Hill went down his inside at Turn 1 and commenced their own battle.

Schumacher was two seconds in front by the end of the opening lap but Hill came back at him, both planning a three-stop strategy for the 81-lap race. Michael, pre-race, perhaps anticipating the need to pass Mansell, had taken off some rear wing to improve his top speed, but now had more of an oversteering car than ideal, while Hill was much happier with the handling of the Williams than in qualifying and hung on a few seconds back.

Just before half distance Schumacher started to push and built a small advantage, only to run wide out of the track's East Terrace corner and clip the wall, damaging the Benetton's right-rear suspension. Hill, however, did not see the impact but only

Right Right Schumacher watches the rest of his home '94 German GP trackside after retiring with engine failure.

Opposite London welcomes home Hill, its new F1 World Champion in 1996.

Below Hill clinched the '96 World Championship at Suzuka in Japan.

Schumacher scrabbling back onto the circuit from the grass. Thinking it could be his only chance, he thrust the Williams down the inside of the following right-hander. Schumacher turned into him, they collided, the Benetton reared up on two wheels, came down right-side up and slithered into the tyre barrier on the outside, out of the race.

Hill limped back to the pits, his left-front top suspension wishbone kinked beyond repair. Devastated, he climbed sadly out. Exactly what the race director had asked not to happen had happened. Many in the sport found it difficult to believe that Schumacher had not seen the Williams coming, and with a stricken car, turning in was his final roll of the dice. Whatever the case, in a season mired in controversy and the death of its greatest driver, there was no appetite for further appeals or investigations. The sport had to move on. Schumacher was now the first German World Champion in F1's 45-year history.

Williams co-founder Sir Patrick Head believes 1994 was Damon Hill's finest year. Normally, after catastrophic accidents, F1 teams get their cars back to analyze what went wrong, if it was clearly a failure on the car. After Senna's accident at Imola, his car was impounded by the Italian authorities. "The senior engineers all came in, we had the data from on board Ayrton's car," Head told F1's *Beyond the Grid* podcast. "Damon came in and was very involved in the analysis of the data because, obviously, he wanted to know what had caused the accident. Damon's personality was very strong in terms of leading the team out of a very difficult time. Obviously, history will have him down as the 1996 World Champion, but his achievements in 1994 were stunning, absolutely stunning."

Schumacher, meanwhile, tried to mitigate the bad taste left by such an ending by dedicating his championship to the late Senna and publicly apologizing to Hill for the earlier derogatory remarks about his ability. The year had been controversial from first to last. The following season Benetton switched from Ford to Renault V10 power and became even stronger, Michael claiming back-to-back championships with Damon runner-up once more. Michael then left to help rebuild Ferrari's struggling team and, in 1996, Damon won the title with Williams as the Hills became the first father/son World Champions in F1 history.

Both Graham and Damon Hill were lauded for their 'determination and character' rather than their ability, something that irked the deep-thinking Damon. But, as racing insiders appreciate, you can't do it without all three. Their amazing family achievement was matched two decades later by Keke and Nico Rosberg, champions in 1982 and 2016 respectively.

Schumacher vs. Häkkinen

Schumacher
91 Grand Prix wins
7 Championships

Häkkinen
20 Grand Prix wins
2 Championships

For a country of five and a half million souls Finland punches well above its weight in representation on the F1 grid. It has produced three World Champions, and the likes of Mika Salo, JJ Lehto, Heikki Kovalainen and Valtteri Bottas. France, the nation that gave us grand prix racing has just one World Champion and Italy only two, the last one coming way back in 1953.

It's a small motorsport world in Finland. Mika Häkkinen was born in Vantaa, Helsinki, on 28 September 1968, and lived in the same street as future Toyota/Ferrari F1 driver Mika Salo. When Häkkinen was six, his father bought a kart belonging to World Rallying ace Henri Toivonen. Mika won the Finnish/Nordic/Swedish FF1600 titles in a car bought from future F1 driver JJ Lehto.

Showing promise in junior formulae in 1988, he was invited to a test for the new Marlboro World Championship Team, which was extending its programme to back young upcoming talents in Formula Vauxhall Lotus, F3 and F3000.

Among the assessors were Marlboro-backed team bosses Ron Dennis, Mike Earle, Hugues de Chaunac, Dick Bennetts and special adviser James Hunt. Häkkinen was in line for a Vauxhall Lotus seat and was given a target time of 1 minute 12.2 seconds by the car's regular driver. Häkkinen hadn't seen Donington before and after a few of laps a disbelieving Hunt was blinking at his stopwatch: 1 minute 10.7 seconds. "Who is that man?" he boomed in his loud, plummy public school voice. "Sign him. Now!"

Häkkinen, with support from the cigarette company, went on to win the Vauxhall Lotus Euroseries and then, in 1990, the British F3 championship. He was one of the favourites to win the year-end Macau GP, until he encountered a certain Michael Schumacher.

The pair had raced each other in karts, and Häkkinen had also driven in a round of the German F3 championship at Hockenheim, and beaten Schumacher.

Macau was run over two legs with aggregated results and Häkkinen won the first from pole, with an almost 3 seconds margin over Schumacher. All he had to do was stay within 3 seconds of Michael in the second leg. Schumacher passed Häkkinen off the start but could not break away. However, on the final lap, with Häkkinen tucked right under his rear wing, Schumacher got out of shape through a flat-out kink on Macau's waterfront.

"I had better straightline speed than him anyway, but he had quite a moment and I jinked right to go past him," Häkkinen remembered. "He moved straight across on me to block but the speed difference was too great and I went into the back of him. A bit of inexperience maybe, but I wasn't happy! I did then wonder about him a little ..."

Häkkinen was out of the race and Schumacher did the last lap without his rear wing and won the event. It was a bitter pill for Mika to swallow but he had already signed with Lotus for F1 in 1991, so didn't dwell on it too long. Schumacher, meanwhile, was destined for another season of sportscar racing ... that is until Jordan driver Bertrand Gachot sprayed CS gas in a London cabbie's face and had to miss races at Her Majesty's Pleasure.

While the Benetton team Schumacher joined after his sensational Jordan debut was in the ascendancy, Team Lotus was headed in the opposite direction. A fifth place in San Marino was Häkkinen's only points finish in 1991, although 1992 was better, Mika outperforming the car as well as teammate

Johnny Herbert to finish in the points six times and ultimately eighth in the World Championship.

McLaren boss Ron Dennis had kept a close eye on Häkkinen ever since that first Marlboro test and now he was impressed again. The team had signed Michael Andretti from IndyCars to partner three-time World Champion Senna in 1993, but with Ayrton not committing until the 11th hour, also offered Häkkinen a reserve driver role and a testing programme.

McLaren and Andretti did not gel and despite Michael achieving a F1 podium in the Italian Grand Prix at Monza, he was sacked by the team in favour of Häkkinen for the final three races.

Mika made a sensational debut in Portugal where he outqualified Senna by 0.05 seconds to put his car on the second row behind the dominant Williams-Renaults. Everyone in F1 thought Mika was very quick but he'd never had decent equipment. Now, they knew. In the race, however, he crashed. In Japan, Häkkinen almost did it again in qualifying, but Senna shaded him by just 0.04 seconds as they pushed to beat Prost's Williams pole time. Ayrton had already signed for Williams in 1994, but a year of Senna vs. Häkkinen would have been an interesting prospect.

Häkkinen then, had the McLaren team leader role for 1994, when he was joined by Martin Brundle. Unfortunately, it was the year of McLaren's ill-fated partnership with Peugeot, which was terminated after just 12 months. The first year of the McLaren-Mercedes partnership was hardly much better and although Häkkinen scored second places at Monza and Suzuka, he posted nine retirements and could do no better than seventh in the Drivers' Championship.

More importantly, he recovered from a serious accident in qualifying for the season-ending Grand Prix in Adelaide, which threatened not only his racing future, but his life. The medical crew stationed on that corner needing to perform an emergency tracheotomy to clear blood from his airways.

"I had a tyre explosion at high speed," Mika explained. "I hit the barrier and cracked my skull. There was a medical team at the corner and a hospital 200m away, so they were positives. In the car I couldn't move, the doctors came and I passed out.

"I was a month in hospital. Ron and Lisa Dennis did everything to protect and help me. I had lots of tests, for all the senses: smell, taste, hearing, everything. I remember the massive headaches and the pain killers. It took me a long time to think about racing. It made me understand how fragile life is. But I had a mission, I'd been racing all my life and I was there to win."

Schumacher's progress in F1 had been spectacular, the German winning back-to-back World Championships with a Ford-powered Benetton B194 and a Renault-powered B195 the year after, before electing to join Ferrari for 1996 in a bid to become the Scuderia's first World Champion since Jody Scheckter in 1979. Häkkinen's good news was that Williams design guru Adrian Newey was on his way to Woking.

In 1997 Schumacher went very close to his first Ferrari title, a win at Suzuka sending him to the Jerez decider a point clear of Jacques Villeneuve. If neither finished, Michael was champion. It was the scenario of Macau and Adelaide all over again, surely Schumacher didn't have the brass neck to try and shove his competition off the road once more …?

Opposite Häkkinen and Ayrton Senna pose for a McLaren team shot at the final race of '93 in Adelaide. Mika got his chance when Michael Andretti was fired post-Monza, and immediately outqualified Senna in Portugal!

Above Häkkinen (9) won his first GP in the controversial conclusion to the '97 season at Jerez, ahead of McLaren teammate David Coulthard.

Left Häkkinen and Schumacher make light contact at Spa's La Source hairpin in '98.

Right Damon Hill, who qualified his Jordan third, nips into the lead as Häkkinen's McLaren and Schumacher's Ferrari dispute territory at Spa. A couple of hundred yards later, David Coulthard's McLaren triggered a 13-car pile-up and race stoppage. Hill won the restarted race to give Eddie Jordan his lone GP win, ahead of teammate Ralf Schumacher.

Villeneuve, having set an identical time to Heinz-Harald Frentzen *and* Schumacher, but, most importantly, set it first, started from pole. No matter, Michael beat him off the line and led the first 47 of the race's 69 laps. Villeneuve then caught him off guard with a late lunge down the inside of Jerez's Dry Sac corner. It's arguable whether Villeneuve would have made the corner without running wide but Schumacher panicked and turned into him.

It evoked memories of his Adelaide incident with Hill and, in the ITV commentary box, Martin Brundle (who had been teammates with Michael at Benetton) exclaimed, "That didn't work, Michael. You hit the wrong part of him, my friend!" The contact was with the Williams left sidepod and it was the Ferrari that suffered damage and was out of the race, while Villeneuve survived and won the title. On the last lap, he let both McLarens by in a pre-arrangement between Williams and McLaren. A McLaren team order had put Mika in front of teammate David Coulthard (because he'd qualified ahead of David) and hence Häkkinen scored his first GP win with a double helping of help!

FIA president Max Mosley launched an inquiry into the Schumacher/Villeneuve incident, after which Michael was disqualified from his second place in the Drivers' Championship, yet Ferrari was allowed to keep his 78 points, without which they would have dropped from second to fifth in the Constructors' Championship, which is what pays the money. A case of making it up as you go along, some claimed. The effect of the action was therefore zero but it did guarantee Schumacher a hefty slap on the wrist via worldwide media condemnation. Schumacher struggled with that, pointing out that both Prost and Senna had

won championships with on-track physicality while being in advantageous positions, and no action had ever been taken.

In 1998, Adrian Newey's McLaren MP4/13 was the class of the field and Häkkinen won four of the first six races. Schumacher and Ferrari hit back strongly, though, and with two races remaining, both men had 80 points and six victories. There was a certain amount of needle between Schumacher and the McLaren team. In a rain-sodden Belgian Grand Prix – one that had started with opening lap carnage out of La Source hairpin when David Coulthard's McLaren had triggered a 13-car accident, Mika Häkkinen spun at the restart and collided with Johnny Herbert taking both out of the race.

Schumacher was leading the restarted race and by lap 24 was 30 seconds up the road from second place Damon Hill when he came up to lap Coulthard in heavy rain. DC was warned that there was a Ferrari about to lap him, slowed down but stayed on the racing line. In such atrocious visibility Schumacher saw the McLaren very late and his closing speed was too great. The impact created a Ferrari three-wheeler which he got back to the pits and then with jaw set, went up the pitlane looking for a fight with the Scotsman. Back at the race, Damon Hill took a much-celebrated first win for the Jordan team and couldn't resist taking the Michael by imitating Schumi's trademark jump on the podium.

All was not lost, though. The momentum was still with Schumacher, and after winning the Italian GP in front of his adoring Tifosi, Ferrari locked out the front row of the Luxembourg Grand Prix at the Nürburgring. It looked like Michael's first Ferrari championship was in reach. But that was not counting a superb drive from Häkkinen, who took the lead after the second pit stops and then

Right Häkkinen is held aloft by teammate David Coulthard and Ferrari's Eddie Irvine after his title win in Japan.

Below Schumacher celebrates his Imola win in 2000, the year he took his third world title and the first with Ferrari.

Opposite Häkkinen, now retired, greets Schumacher on the grid for the '05 Hungarian GP. There was always mutual respect between the pair.

extended his advantage over Schumacher before having the luxury of backing off in the closing stages. Michael looked shell-shocked. Going to the Suzuka finale, Mika now led by four points and a second place behind Michael would give him his first World Championship.

Schumacher took pole with Häkkinen alongside, but then disaster, the Ferrari stalled on the grid. The field was released for another parade lap and Michael had to start from the back of the grid. That took the pressure off Häkkinen, and a subsequent Schumacher puncture and retirement confirmed Mika as the second Finnish World Champion, with eight wins over the season to Michael's six. Mika won back-to-back titles in 1999 as Schumacher broke his leg in a mid-season crash at Silverstone and missed six races, the championship again going down to a last-round decider, this time Mika getting the better of Schumacher's Ferrari teammate, Eddie Irvine.

Schumacher finally achieved his ambition of winning a championship with Ferrari (his first of five) in 2000 when he won nine times, including the first three races of the season and the last four. In between, though, Häkkinen fought him hard, with Spa prominent. It produced one of F1's most replayed overtaking moves.

Schumacher, expecting more rain than actually materialized, had set the Ferrari up with more downforce, but with five laps to go on a dry track, with Häkkinen right behind him, was paying for that with less straightline speed on the long Kemmel straight which follows the daunting Eau Rouge section.

Häkkinen was less than impressed when Schumacher gave him 'the chop' at over 200mph as he tried to go inside. A wheel-over-wheel incident there would have resulted in a serious accident. Mika channelled his anger into an incredible pass on the following lap when they caught up with back marker Ricardo Zonta. Michael went left around Zonta and Mika, with millimetre precision, went right and passed both of them. It was extraordinarily brave. If Zonta had suddenly moved right to give Schumacher more room …

The laid-back Häkkinen was never prone to public outbursts and, afterwards, calmly but firmly let Michael know what he thought of his dangerous manoeuvre. Michael, nodding, took it on board. They never had anything but the utmost respect for each other. After fighting out three consecutive seasons, Schumacher admitted that he regarded Häkkinen more highly than any other competitor he ever faced and, tellingly, neither ever publicly criticized the other.

For Mika though, his motivation was on the wane. In 2001, a ban on beryllium impacted the Mercedes Ilmor engines and while Schumacher won his fourth world title with a further nine wins, Mika took the chequered flag just twice. He fell to fifth in the championship standings with McLaren teammate David Coulthard runner-up. Son Hugo was born that year and, having made his decision at Monaco, his home, 'The Flying Finn' retired at the end of the year.

Alonso vs. Hamilton

Alonso
32 Grand Prix wins
2 Championships

Hamilton
103 Grand Prix wins
7 Championships

Opposite 2001 Benetton-Renault launch at St Mark's Square in Venice with drivers Jenson Button, Giancarlo Fisichella, Fernando Alonso and Mark Webber.

Right Lewis Hamilton wins his first GP2 Series race in 2006 at Nürburgring, Germany.

Fernando Alonso and Lewis Hamilton were together at McLaren for just a single season, so their intra-team rivalry did not last long. But their short combustible time together would have long-term consequences for the team. Fittingly, perhaps, Fernando is the son of an explosives expert.

Alonso was born 29 July 1981, in Oviedo, a city in the Asturias province of northern Spain. He was every centimetre the precocious talent, Fernando was driving karts shortly after his third birthday. His ability with a kart was transferred seamlessly to cars and he won the Euro Open by Nissan title at 17, before moving on to Formula 3000 and the Minardi-backed Astromega team.

Those performances earned Alonso a Minardi test and reserve driver deal for 2000, from where he was promoted to the race team in 2001. Minardi was a tail-end team who gave valuable track mileage to up-and-coming stars, with Mark Webber, Giancarlo Fisichella and Jarno Trulli driving for them before moving on to front-running teams. It was not until Alonso joined Renault that he could show his full potential.

Having impressed as a Renault test driver in 2002, he was given a full race seat in 2003 at Jenson Button's expense, and in the year's second race, in Malaysia, he set a new record (subsequently beaten by Sebastian Vettel and Charles Leclerc) for the youngest F1 driver ever to take pole position. And when he won the Hungarian Grand Prix later the same year, he set a new record as the youngest GP winner in F1 history (subsequently beaten by Vettel, Leclerc and Max Verstappen).

It was an era of Bridgestone-shod Ferrari domination, but new regulations for 2005 (that lasted just a year) banned in-race tyre changing. French team Renault naturally ran the French-made Michelin tyres and they were now competitive with Bridgestone, who had been tailoring their tyres for Ferrari for the last five seasons. Alonso took full advantage to claim six wins, 14 podiums and usurp Emerson Fittipaldi's record (25 years and 273 days when he won in 1972) as the youngest World Champion in the sport's history. Alonso was 24 years and 57 days. The youngest F1 champion is now Sebastian Vettel (23 years and 133 days in 2010), with Hamilton second (23 years and 300 days in 2008).

At the Japanese Grand Prix that year, Alonso had a secret meeting with McLaren boss Ron Dennis and agreed to a three-year contract with McLaren Mercedes starting more than a year down the road, in 2007. Already, Fernando had the ability to cause considerable turbulence within teams. He defended his world title successfully in 2006, but the Renault technical director at the time, Pat Symonds, recalls that he was not averse to spitting the dummy. In one famous outburst, Alonso claimed that there were a "handful of people (at Renault) who don't want me to take No.1 to McLaren."

"That's partly why he was never very popular in the team," Symonds says. "He just went off on one and really turned people against him, because they were working super-hard and it was a really good team. Totally out of the blue there was this tirade to the press, not to us, about how we weren't supporting his championship bid. It was almost self-destructive. Everyone in the team wanted to win the championship but, honestly, if we'd won the constructors' and not the drivers' title there'd have been several people saying, 'Yeah, that's fine …'

"And then he left for McLaren and didn't even come to our championship celebration. He gave a bottle of wine to everyone in the factory at the end of 2005, but at the end of 2006 gave them to the people at McLaren!"

Alonso had been talking to Dennis about potential team-mates for 2007, and knowing that Hamilton was on his way to winning the GP2 championship said that McLaren couldn't win the Constructors' Championship with a rookie. It's a Formula 1 truism that whenever a leading driver is complementary about a teammate, they know they can beat them. Fernando's preferred choice was countryman Pedro de la Rosa, who had replaced the cavalier Juan Pablo Montoya (a poor fit for McLaren) midway through the previous year and finished second in Hungary. Maybe Fernando was being genuine … or maybe he'd watched some of Hamilton's remarkable GP2 performances.

Whatever, McLaren plumped for Lewis and they were thrown together. Back in those days, practically unlimited testing meant that by the time the season kicked off in Australia, Hamilton had around 6,000 miles under his belt and was as well prepared as any rookie could be. He'd also been part of the McLaren set-up for almost 10 years, supported by Ron Dennis from karting upwards. In many respects, although he was a defending two-time World Champion, it was Alonso who felt like the new boy.

From the very beginning Lewis's pace was a match for Fernando's and it was not long before there was tension. Alonso was adamant that he'd joined as No.1 driver and Dennis was equally adamant that McLaren did not favour one driver over another. Team orders, if need be, would come later. Alonso won

round two in Malaysia but when Hamilton beat him in Fernando's home race at Barcelona two races later, it was his third successive second place and the rookie led the championship by two points.

Monaco was next and it was a second victory for Alonso, who started from pole. Hamilton, however, thought he had stronger race pace and was annoyed to be told to drop back from Alonso. "I'm not here to finish second," he told Dennis.

Next time out in Montreal, Lewis won his first grand prix and, a week later, began his long love affair with winning in the United States by clinching victory at the USGP at Indianapolis. Alonso's third win came in round 11, the European GP at the Nürburgring, after which the championship looked like this: Hamilton, 70 points; Alonso, 68; Felipe Massa (Ferrari), 59; 4, Kimi Räikkönen (Ferrari), 52.

Mercedes actually used the duo's much-publicized tussle for a funny television advert where both drivers race each other to check in to a hotel, grab the lift, get to their hotel room first to the tune of 'Anything You Can Do, I Can Do Better'. The ending involved Mika Häkkinen, Mercedes' last World Champion beating them both. But things were about to get serious.

In the background, McLaren chief designer Mike Coughlan had been leaked 700 pages of Ferrari technical information by disaffected Ferrari employee Nigel Stepney. Unbelievably, Coughlan's wife had the documents duplicated at a local copy shop, which just happened to be staffed by a Ferrari fan, who telephoned Maranello. You couldn't make it up …

Dennis put the original fire out by claiming that the information had not gone further than Coughlan, who was sacked. But McLaren's season imploded in Hungary.

Opposite Fernando Alonso and Renault celebrate their second successive World Championship at Interlagos, Brazil, in 2006.

Above Left to right: Test and reserve drivers Gary Paffett (left) and Pedro de la Rosa (right) flank the new McLaren line-up of reigning double champion Alonso and a rookie Lewis Hamilton ahead of the 2007 season.

Left Alonso sprays the bubbly on the Spanish GP podium, but he finished his home race third, ten seconds adrift of teammate Hamilton, who now led the championship four races in.

Right Alonso kicks up the dust as
he disputes Turn 2 of the Spanish GP
with Hamilton, ahead of Ferrari's Kimi
Räikkönen. Pole man Felipe Massa
has already gone.

The rules at the time required cars to start the race with their
qualifying fuel loads and do a number of 'fuel burn' laps in the
session to get down to a lighter weight at the end of the session
when grid time were set. It was an advantage to be first out and the
McLaren drivers took it in turns.

In Hungary, it was Alonso's turn but Hamilton went to the end of
the pitlane first and, when instructed to let Fernando past, did not
comply, using the excuse that Räikkönen was too close behind him.

Alonso, furious, dropped back to almost a lap behind Hamilton
and then pitted first for his fresh tyres. Once they'd been fitted,
however, he sat in the pits with Hamilton stacked behind him, just
long enough to ensure that Hamilton would not have time to get
his qualifying lap in. Sure enough, Alonso took pole at what is a
Monaco-like track for overtaking.

The problem had been initiated by Hamilton but Lewis's father,
Anthony Hamilton, then lobbied race stewards who, for some
reason, got involved in what was basically an internal McLaren
issue. They awarded Fernando a five-place grid penalty and
Alonso went postal.

For some time he had been telling Dennis that he and Hamilton
should not be racing each other and that they risked losing the
championships to Ferrari if they didn't control Hamilton who, he felt,
had many more opportunities to come.

By this stage, it had emerged that the 'Spygate' saga had
run much deeper through the McLaren organization than
previously claimed. On race morning, Alonso, still furious, had a
blazing row with Dennis, during which he said that if the team did
not control Hamilton and right the wrong of the previous day by

allegedly ensuring that Hamilton ran out of fuel during the race, then Fernando would disclose incriminating emails to FIA president Max Mosley.

Dennis, unsure what to do and considering stopping Alonso from racing, phoned Mosley himself and admitted the conversation. Mosley advised Dennis to allow Alonso to compete. Hamilton, predictably, won from pole and Alonso finished fourth from his sixth on the grid.

Some believed that Dennis had been the architect of his own downfall by phoning Mosley. It led to a second, more detailed inquiry into the Spygate shenanigans but, in his biography, Mosley claimed that he already knew about the emails because Alonso had told his manager, Flavio Briatore, who had told his good buddy Bernie Ecclestone, who naturally had passed it along to Max.

A month later the resulting investigation led to McLaren being thrown out of the Constructors' Championship and given the biggest fine in sporting history, $100 million. Renault faced a similar charge of possessing McLaren intellectual property and got away with it. A PR shot of Mosley and Dennis shaking hands on the steps of McLaren's motor home/brand centre at Spa was orchestrated, during which Mosley allegedly told Dennis, "$5 million is for the offence and $95 million is for being a ****!" Mosley, however, claimed it was Ecclestone who said it. Mosley, who never enjoyed the best of relationships with Dennis, also said that he was all for throwing McLaren out of F1 but that Ecclestone persuaded him to go the fine route.

Despite Alonso having retracted what he said to Dennis, claiming it was a heat-of-the-moment thing, Alonso's position

within the team was now untenable. Severance negotiations were held that would see him return to Renault for 2008. Alonso won at Monza and also beat Hamilton at Spa, where there was more aggravation between the pair.

"I got a great start and was right behind Massa, who was second as we drove into La Source hairpin," Hamilton explained, "I pulled myself up alongside Fernando as we went in. After everything that had happened I didn't think he could do anything else that could surprise me, but he did! He swung his car across mine and effectively forced me off the track. He left me no room whatsoever. I can accept hard racing but I felt Fernando's move was unfair."

There were two points between them after Belgium but that became a 12-point advantage for Hamilton when he drove a fine race to win a soaking Japanese Grand Prix at Fuji as Alonso aquaplaned off the road and crashed. With two rounds to go, the championship position was: Hamilton, 107; Alonso, 95; Räikkönen, 90.

With points awarded 10-8-6-5-4-3-2-1 to the top eight finishers, it seemed unfeasible that a McLaren driver would not win the championship. But there followed two bizarre races, both won by Räikkönen, allowing the Finn to take the title with 110 points to the 109 of both Hamilton and Alonso!

Some claim that Mosley believed the sport would be a laughing stock if Hamilton or Alonso won the championship after the team had been fined $100 million for receiving technical information from its nearest rival. The inference being that McLaren was quietly told that if they wanted to continue in Formula 1,

Opposite top McLaren boss Ron Dennis first met Lewis Hamilton at the '95 Autosport Awards in London, when the 10-year-old told him that one day he would drive one of his cars. Twelve years on, Dennis was tasked with trying to control Hamilton's burning desire to win the World Championship in his first season, against a feisty reigning double champion. It did not end well …

Opposite bottom The McLarens of Alonso and Hamilton lead into the first corner of the '07 Italian GP at Monza, a race won by the Spaniard.

Left Never say never: Alonso's return to McLaren in 2015 after their divorce circumstances in '07, proved that all things in life are possible …

they needed to ensure that such a thing did not happen. The governance of the sport in those days was very much a Mosley fiefdom, and if he wanted to make it happen, he could.

Asked about it five years later, Hamilton responded, "I didn't know at the time, but I do now. It's not something I can talk about."

In China, Hamilton led convincingly on a wet track until it started to dry and he was passed by Räikkönen. Lewis told the team that his tyres were finished and he needed to pit. The pit wall, however, told him that he was doing a great job and needed to stay out a little longer. Which puzzled Lewis, as he'd fallen 9 seconds off the pace of his best lap … The official line was that McLaren was monitoring weather reports and trying to ensure it made the right tyre choice to avoid an additional stop.

By the time Lewis pitted, his rear tyres were down to the canvas and he had no grip whatsoever, but he couldn't see the full state of them from the cockpit because his mirrors were dirty from spray. He ended up beached in the world's only pitlane gravel trap.

Hamilton was still a strong favourite going into the Interlagos season finale, needing just a top five finish to ensure that Räikkönen could not win the title. He qualified second behind Massa's Ferrari but was also beaten off the line by Räikkönen and passed by Alonso at the Senna Esses. He then locked up into Turn 4 trying to re-pass Fernando and dropped to ninth. Then came a brief gearbox glitch, a somewhat bizarre three-stop strategy by the team and a need to manage the engine and run lower revs, all contributing to an eventual seventh place and just two points.

Alonso, meanwhile, was strangely off the pace all race, finishing almost a minute behind the Ferraris. At Maranello,

meanwhile, a delayed final pit stop for Felipe Massa allowed Räikkönen through to win the title by that single point.

For drama and intrigue, 2007 ranks right up there with 1976 and 2021. A rookie Hamilton so very nearly won the championship in his debut season and fully deserved to do so. Alonso then embarked on a career trajectory of being in the wrong car, although in 2010 it so nearly came right. Had the opportunities arisen he could have won a similar number of titles to Schumacher and, later, Hamilton. There are those at Ferrari who believe that Alonso was better than Schumacher, which makes Hamilton's 2007 achievement all the more remarkable.

Fernando's 2015 return to the McLaren team, who he had helped saddle with enormous debt, really did prove that anything in life is possible …

Vettel vs. Webber

Vettel
53 Grand Prix wins
4 Championships

Webber
9 Grand Prix wins
0 Championships

The pairing of German 'wunderkind' Sebastian Vettel with straight-talking Aussie bloke Mark Webber at Red Bull in 2009 gave rise to some highly charged moments over the following five seasons.

Webber, born 27 August 1976, was the elder statesman. He had impressed in Australian Formula Ford before coming to England and winning the prestigious Formula Ford Festival, previously won by such luminaries as Jenson Button, Johnny Herbert, Roberto Moreno and Jan Magnussen. That earned him a phone call and then support from Mercedes motorsport boss Norbert Haug, who helped fund Webber's British F3 programme as well as signing him for the Mercedes sportscar team. Ultimately that relationship soured when Webber had the scariest of experiences at Le Mans in 1999. "I think we had a weak engine, and that in turn made us run the car with very little downforce," he recalled in his autobiography *Aussie Grit*. "That was maybe not the avenue we would have liked to have endeavoured, but we did. Taking downforce off the car made more speed in the straights, but it made the car a little more susceptible to instability at high speeds, on the front end. And obviously that's where it takes off." And take off it did down the Mulsanne straight. He concentrated on single-seaters for the next 14 years after that.

Australian entrepreneur and new Minardi team owner Paul Stoddart invested $1.1 million in Webber's career. In a fairytale F1 debut with Minardi in 2002 he finished fifth in his home Australian GP after Ralf Schumacher laid waste to eight cars in an opening lap accident. Webber and Stoddart even sneaked onto the podium afterwards to acknowledge the crowd, but that was as good as it got in 2002.

For most of his career, like his great friend Fernando Alonso, Mark Webber was never in the right place at the right time. Some impressive performances for Jaguar in 2003 attracted interest from Frank Williams, whose team Webber joined in 2004. Many envisioned the kind of relationship that Alan Jones and Williams enjoyed over four years beginning in the late 1970s, but Williams was on a downward path and it didn't work out for Mark, who had just a single podium to show for his two years with the team when he left to join the young Red Bull Racing team for 2007. At the same time, another Flavio Briatore-managed driver, Fernando Alonso, was winning back-to-back titles with Renault. Adept at saying the wrong thing at the wrong time – Flavio once described future World Champion Jenson Button as so slow he was a "milepost" – he never stopped reminding Webber of Alonso's success.

It was also in 2007 that 19-year-old Sebastian Vettel, born 3 July 1987, made his Formula 1 debut with BMW-Sauber in the US Grand Prix at Indianapolis. After a successful karting career, Vettel became a Red Bull protégé, dominating the Formula BMW championship and was leading the Formula Renault 3.5 series when Robert Kubica had a huge accident in the Canadian GP in Montreal and was unfit to drive the following weekend. At 19 years and 349 days, Vettel became the youngest driver ever to score an F1 point (a record he lost to Max Verstappen in 2015) when he finished eighth at Indianapolis, crossing the finish line just half a second behind Webber's Red Bull. With their characteristic hire-and-fire management style the Red Bull organization then dropped American Scott Speed from the Toro Rosso junior team and put Vettel in the car for the second half of the year, in preparation for a full season in 2008.

Christian Horner was hoping for a debut victory for the Red Bull team in 2008, but it was the Adrian Newey-designed Toro Rosso STR3 that got there first, at Monza. After a superb pole position (when Vettel became the youngest polesitter in F1 history – 21 years and 72 days) in wet conditions, few in the paddock thought he would make the podium at the end of the 53 laps. A mature drive from Vettel that belied his age proved them wrong. It earned him a promotion to the senior team alongside Webber for 2009.

Another Antipodean driver, the late Chris Amon, is hailed by many to be the best driver never to win a grand prix, the Kiwi missing out so often due to bad luck. Webber, after seven years at the sport's highest level without finding himself in a race-winning car, looked as if he might have inherited Amon's mantle. Design ace Adrian Newey had already been poached from McLaren by Red Bull team principal Christian Horner and there was much optimism about Newey's RB5 chassis for 2009. But, over the winter, Webber, riding a bicycle in his charity Tasmanian Challenge, was hit by a Nissan Patrol SUV which broke his right leg. The Tasmanian accident happened on 22 November and Red Bull had a pre-season test scheduled for 11 February, which he was determined to be at.

Helping Webber through his less successful years in F1 was his ability to regularly outperform his teammates, something he had done at Red Bull in 2008 alongside 13-time grand prix winner David Coulthard. "I just couldn't live with you" the Scot admitted when he called time on his F1 career at the end of that season. That opened up the vacancy for Vettel. Sebastian was tipped as "the

new Michael Schumacher" or "baby Schumi" and also the man who would finish Webber's career. Were these the words of a hostile German media? No, they were uttered by Red Bull owner Dietrich Mateschitz's right-hand man, Helmut Marko. Webber thought it an odd statement to make before they'd even raced together …

As it turned out, Newey's new Red Bull was not immediately the class of the field. When Honda pulled out of F1 at the end of 2008 amid the global financial crisis, Ross Brawn bought the Brackley-based team for £1 with Honda providing a rudimentary operating budget for the first season and, crucially, Mercedes providing an engine. A highly effective car with a trick diffuser that rival teams protested in vain, allowed Jenson Button to win six of the first seven races, the only interruption being Vettel's win – the first for the senior Red Bull team – in China, where Webber followed him home second.

Early season, Webber was struggling with his leg, but wasn't about to let on. It was the German Grand Prix in July before he first outqualified Vettel, going on to win the race, despite a drive-through penalty for a coming-together with Rubens Barrichello at the start. Psychologically it was a breakthrough for Webber, proving to himself that he could get the job done. He had scored his debut victory in his 130th race, 232 days after breaking his leg.

Red Bull came on strong in the second half of the season but Brawn's start proved decisive and Button clinched the championship in Brazil. But with RB6 on Newey's drawing board, things looked good for 2010. Vettel drew first blood in a Malaysian Grand Prix 1-2 but Webber hit back strongly to win the Spanish GP. High-speed corners were always a strength and Webber was elated when the team telemetry proved that he was flat-out

Opposite David Coulthard with Webber at the launch of Red Bull's RB4 in 2008, which would be Coulthard's last F1 season.

Above The famous digit. Vettel led the 2010 Championship for the first time after the final round in Abu Dhabi, clinching the first of four successive world titles with Red Bull.

Left Same venue, same result ... Webber soaks Vettel in champagne after a 1–2 in the '09 Abu Dhabi GP at Yas Marina.

Left Future Channel 4 commentators and analysts Webber and Coulthard battle it out in the '07 German GP at Nürburgring.

Above Webber and Vettel make contact in the 2010 Turkish GP.

Right Vettel, on his way back to the pits, makes it clear what he thinks of Webber's approach, despite the common consensus being that Sebastian was at fault.

Opposite Webber achieved a life's ambition by winning at Monaco in 2010, and celebrates with a flip into the pool at Red Bull's Energy Station.

through Barcelona's tricky Turn 9. A week later he realized a lifetime's ambition when he won the Monaco Grand Prix from pole, after which he and Vettel shared the championship lead with 78 points to Fernando Alonso's 75 at Ferrari.

Things were now getting prickly in the intra-team rivalry. In his autobiography, Webber writes, "To my way of thinking, if you get done on the day you should take it on the chin, but Seb's arrogance meant that he simply couldn't comprehend how things had gone wrong. Guillaume 'Rocky' Rocquelin, his engineer, was the only one who would tell it to him straight. I'm sure some of it was down to his youthfulness but the team's executive management repeatedly allowed him to get away with it. He was treated like a favourite son, which meant he would throw his toys out of the pram from time to time when he didn't get his own way. I cut him some slack because I got to know his family and liked them. You could tell they were decent people with a good set of values."

After Monaco, Seb felt that there had to be a reason he had lost the last two races to his teammate – he wanted Webber's chassis. Helmut Marko covered the demand by saying that Vettel's was cracked, an assertion viewed with scepticism elsewhere in the team. At the next race in Turkey, Webber was unimpressed when a new Red Bull rear wing went on Vettel's car first despite the Aussie having won the previous two races from pole. In those days, aerodynamic 'F-ducts' needed setting up, which took time, and Webber got his wing just in time for qualifying, in which he bested Vettel again, by almost half a second.

A close race between the two Red Bulls and the two McLarens ended controversially with contact between Vettel and Webber as Sebastian tried to pass Mark, who had led for most of the race. The incident was clearly Vettel's fault, something that most of the team, including team principal Horner realized, so Webber was dismayed when Marko laid blame at Webber's door to the German-speaking media. Upon which Horner's opinion appeared to make a U-turn. Another thing that deeply irked Webber was that Vettel was given permission to miss the team debrief, something deemed very important to preparation for upcoming races and which sometimes took two hours.

Webber was now convinced that the team had an agenda and that it didn't include having "a washed up old Australian dog" beating its new wonderboy. After an avalanche of texted support, he took the advice of a captain of industry and penned a letter direct to Mateschitz, which did not sit well with Horner. Discussing what he felt was Vettel's sense of entitlement with Horner, Christian told him privately that the problem was that Sebastian was reading straight from the pages of the Michael Schumacher playbook. Vettel had three childhood idols, all Michaels – Schumacher, Jordan and Jackson.

The following race in Canada was one of the team's weaker performances but Webber was told to stay behind Vettel as they finished in P4 and 5. As if the perceived favouritism wasn't bad enough, a Renault engineer had let slip that when the engines were dyno-tested, the stronger one went to Seb's side of the garage. Webber's doubts, which some were starting to call paranoia, were insufficient to prevent him extending his Red Bull contract at the same time. When you've waited so long for such a cockpit, you don't give it up ...

Vettel won in Valencia while Webber had an awful accident in which he somersaulted after being launched over the back of Heikki Kovalainen's Lotus. After a 10-year break from his Mercedes aviating, he was fortunate to miss a bridge and come down right-side up, emerging unscathed despite hitting the wall so hard that he moved concrete barriers several metres and broke the brake pedal.

Then came the British Grand Prix, effectively a home race for the team despite it racing under an Austrian licence. A new front wing, said to be potentially worth a couple of tenths, was taken off Webber's car and given to Vettel for qualifying when Sebastian damaged his own in practice, leaving Mark furious. The team explanation was that Vettel had been quicker in final practice, which Webber said was disingenuous because, after issues on Friday, he was doing heavily fuelled longer runs. Vettel outqualified him by 0.143 seconds. "The slogan says Red Bull gives you wings," Webber said, "but they don't. At least not both of us …"

Driving the car that Vettel had discarded after Monaco – remember, the cracked chassis – Webber beat Vettel off the line and won the race. When he was congratulated over the radio on the slowdown lap, he came back with his famous, "Not bad for a No.2 driver …" Again, it caused discord within the team despite Webber insisting later that it was merely a bit of wry Aussie humour and not intended to prolong the feud.

When Webber won in Hungary after Vettel was hit with a penalty for losing concentration and failing to maintain the proper distance behind the Safety Car, the Aussie led the championship once again. But it didn't help things when he

Right Red Bull title protagonists Webber and Vettel before the 2010 Championship showdown in Abu Dhabi.

Below Vettel on the Abu Dhabi podium with McLaren drivers Lewis Hamilton and Jenson Button after winning the race and the World Championship in 2010.

Opposite "Multi 21, Seb?" A disenchanted Webber waits to hear teammate Vettel's reasons for ignoring team orders in a frosty press conference at the 2013 Malaysian GP.

2013 FORMULA 1 PETRONAS MALAYSIA GRAND PRIX

fell off a mountain bike and damaged a shoulder, having to race at Suzuka with pain-killing injections.

Post Japan, the score was Webber, 220 points, Alonso and Vettel 206, with the World Championship scoring system now 25-18-15-12-10-8-6-4-2-1. Korea, though, was a disastrous race for the Red Bull drivers. On a wet track, searching for additional grip off line, Webber spun out. Meanwhile, Vettel's engine blew and Alonso's Ferrari won the race. The score was now: Alonso, 231; Webber, 220; Hamilton, 210; and Vettel, 206.

At the penultimate round in Brazil it was a different story and Red Bull hit back with a 1-2 at Interlagos, Vettel ahead of Webber. This was the point at which the team could have imposed team orders, with Christian Horner recommending to Mateschitz that they should back Webber. There had been a really awkward team meeting on race morning when Marko said, no, Vettel should be left in the fight for as long as possible. They therefore headed to the Abu Dhabi season shoot-out with Webber eight points adrift of Alonso but seven ahead of Vettel.

Vettel, the outsider with nothing to lose, drove superbly to take pole position and win the race. Webber, by contrast, could only qualify fifth, his worst showing since the opening race of the season. After his pit stop, he found himself jumped by Alonso. However, Ferrari had given up track position to get in front of their closest championship rival Webber, forgetting they had the Red Bull of Vettel to factor in. Both of them lost time stuck behind Vitaly Petrov's Renault and came home a miserable seventh and eighth. Vettel was champion by four points after topping the table for the first time all year, the final score: Vettel, 256; Alonso, 252; Webber, 242.

It would be the first of four successive titles for Sebastian as Red Bull enjoyed a period of domination. Webber was not mentally ready for 2011 after his disappointment and 2010 remained his best challenge. He felt increasingly undermined over the next three years, culminating in the infamous 'Multi 21' incident at the 2013 Malaysian GP. With Webber in front with 12 laps remaining, the team issued the order, which meant that car 2 (Webber) should finish ahead of car 1 (Vettel). But Sebastian chose to ignore it and there followed one of F1's most uncomfortable podiums and post-race press conferences.

The relationship between the two drivers was always tense but Webber was magnanimous enough to say, "None of it should detract from the job Seb did. I can say with absolute honesty that he was a better all-round F1 driver than I ever was. I'd just like to have had a crack at him 10 years earlier."

Hamilton vs. Rosberg

Hamilton

103 Grand Prix wins

7 Championships

Rosberg

23 Grand Prix wins

1 Championship

When Lewis Hamilton left McLaren to join Mercedes for the 2013 season he rekindled a friendly rivalry with Nico Rosberg that dated back almost 20 years, to their karting days. It would become less friendly as the years rolled on.

At the time, the Mercedes team was three years into its Formula 1 return as a works entity and could boast just a single victory, Rosberg winning the 2012 Chinese GP. Many considered it a strange move from Hamilton. Yes, Ross Brawn and Niki Lauda had both played their part in recruiting the man thought to be the equal of Fernando Alonso and possibly Sebastian Vettel, but who had gone four seasons at McLaren without repeating his championship success of 2008. But there was another factor.

Hamilton had done some late-night partying, reported in a tabloid newspaper, and in an effort to hang on to a driving asset he had supported for over a decade, McLaren boss Ron Dennis intervened. Knowing that Mercedes and Hamilton's management were in negotiations, he had warned Stuttgart's Dieter Zetsche that such headlines were no problem for an independent team like McLaren, but potentially a liability for a corporate organization such as Mercedes.

The tactic backfired. When it reached Hamilton's ears, he was furious and some claim that it actually tipped the balance in him putting pen to paper for Mercedes.

He and Rosberg had both been highly successful karters, driving for the same team under the eye of Italian karting guru Dino Chiesa, who has said that Hamilton was the quicker, more instinctive driver but that Rosberg was very close and the more analytical of the two.

They came from very different backgrounds. Hamilton, born 7 January 1985, was from a Stevenage council estate. Father Anthony worked three jobs to pay for Lewis's early karting exploits, one of which was erecting 'For Sale' boards for an estate agent friend at 50p a go. Rosberg, born 27 June of the same year, is the son of Keke Rosberg, the 1982 World Champion with Williams, privately schooled and brought up in Monte Carlo.

At just 10 years old, Hamilton was present at the annual Autosport Awards gala evening at the Grosvenor House hotel in London's Park Lane to collect his cadet karting award. He had marched up to Ron Dennis's table and told him, "One day, I want to drive one of your cars." Three years later he became part of McLaren's young driver programme, so leaving for Mercedes was like leaving family after 13 years. Many thought he was crazy to leave a proven championship winner.

Mercedes was making progress and, although Red Bull Racing was still the dominant force – Sebastian Vettel won a fourth consecutive title and the last nine races of 2013 – the Brackley-based team claimed three victories. Hamilton finished fourth in the championship and Rosberg sixth, Lewis winning in Budapest and Nico taking Monaco and Silverstone.

It was all-change in 2014 when F1's hybrid era began. Mercedes had invested heavily in the new technology. The paddock rumour mill suggested that they were streets ahead. Pre-season, Hamilton and Rosberg could be had at 16/1 and 25/1 respectively for the championship. Very good business for anyone brave enough! The rumour mill was right and Mercedes totally dominated the next three seasons before Ferrari got its act a little more together in

2017–18. The Merc's competitiveness drastically upped the stakes in their personal rivalry, the pair fighting it out, sometimes bitterly, over the next three seasons. It's a rivalry that has been likened to Senna vs. Prost. The reality is that Lewis and Nico were much more evenly matched than Ayrton and Alain ever were. Rosberg, using the analytical strengths outlined by his karting boss all those years ago, was able to take Hamilton's telemetry and identify areas where he could improve, the reverse was not always the case.

Although Hamilton was viewed as the quicker single-lap driver, he only shaded their qualifying battles 42–36 over the 78 races they contested as teammates over four seasons at Mercedes. However, Hamilton's racecraft was indisputably better.

In 2014 Rosberg took the season-opener in Australia, where Hamilton retired, but Lewis hit back in Malaysia and then in round three in Bahrain they fought a tough battle which got physical, Nico feeling he'd been pushed off a couple of times at Turn 4. There was more controversy when Hamilton accused Rosberg of using engine modes that were banned by Mercedes to give him a performance edge. Nico then accused Lewis of exactly the same thing when Hamilton defended a closing Rosberg to win in Spain and go to the head of the championship table.

There was a further squabble in Monaco when Rosberg set a quicker time than Hamilton on his first Q3 run after Lewis had been faster all weekend. Then, as they started their final runs with Nico ahead, Rosberg missed his braking for Mirabeau, shot down the escape road and caused the session to be yellow-flagged, which ruined Hamilton's lap after Lewis had set the quickest first sector.

Although it was a mistake rarely seen in F1 qualifying, the ruse was much more skilfully executed than Michael Schumacher's attempt at cementing his pole by spinning at Rascasse eight years earlier, which earned Michael universal condemnation. Ironically, one of Schumacher's biggest detractors when that happened was a certain Keke Rosberg! Toto Wolff wouldn't be drawn, he had two Mercedes on the front row, but Hamilton said, "I should have known that was going to happen ..." It was evident that their relationship had soured.

In Hungary, Rosberg took pole and Hamilton faced a back-of-the-grid start after his car developed a fuel leak in qualifying. Lewis made quick progress through the field, aided by a Safety Car, which shuffled the order and put Lewis ahead of Nico on the road. Rosberg, however, had made his pit stop and was on fresher tyres. When the team informed Hamilton and asked him to move over, Lewis refused, claiming that Nico wasn't close enough and that he'd move over if Rosberg caught him.

The pair finally came together in the Belgian Grand Prix at Spa. Rosberg made a half-hearted move on Hamilton at Les Combes, leaving his nose in rather than back out of a move at the chicane at the top of the hill. He felt it was time that he fought fire with fire but the move was never on and revealed what many of his detractors felt – that he could qualify and lead with the fastest car, but when it came to overtaking he wasn't in the same league as his teammate. When Lewis turned in, Nico suffered a damaged front wing that required a pit stop, but Lewis got a puncture and was faced with a slow drive back to the pits on one of the calendar's longest laps, putting him out of contention.

Opposite When Rosberg joined Mercedes for 2010, he got the better of Michael Schumacher, who returned to F1 after a three-year sabbatical.

Above Rosberg and Hamilton became Mercedes teammates in 2013 in a partnership that would last four seasons.

Left The former karting teammates and rivals at the launch of the 2014 Mercedes W04.

Right Rosberg heads Hamilton at the start of the 2016 Spanish GP. A couple of hundred yards later, it all went badly wrong …

The championship only went down to the wire in Abu Dhabi, because of a much-pilloried Bernie Ecclestone idea that double points should be on offer for the final round, to try to ensure that any title fight lasted as long as possible to increase media interest.

Hamilton secured his second world title when he won the race with Rosberg hampered by an energy recovery system failure that saw him limp home 14th. Nico was sporting in defeat, with Hamilton finishing up 67 points clear with 11 wins to his teammate's five.

The 'easiest' of Hamilton's seasons alongside Rosberg was 2015 when he had his third world title wrapped up by the US Grand Prix in Austin, always a favourite venue for him. He needed a victory to retain his championship and ran Rosberg wide at Turn 1 to take the lead, much to Nico's annoyance. It was now all a bit personal and Rosberg did his level best to chase Hamilton down. It was a close-run thing until Nico made a mistake at Turn 12 and Lewis took the win.

In the cooldown room before heading out onto the podium, the acrimony was clear for all to see when Hamilton, pointedly, threw the second-place cap in Nico's direction, without looking at him. Rosberg, still steaming about the Turn 1 incident, threw it right back at him, his face betraying his anger. On the podium, Nico did not participate in any champagne celebrations. "It was a step too far," he claimed. It was only a couple of races after Suzuka, where Nico took pole but Lewis came down his inside at Turn 2 and ran him wide on the exit, costing Rosberg two more places.

Throughout his F1 career Hamilton has earned a reputation for fairness in combat but such is his skill and, throughout his time at Mercedes his car advantage, that he's barely needed to be anything else. Rosberg had an interesting take on Hamilton's defending and overtaking: "Lewis is so good at that," he said. "He can go to that grey area without ever stepping over. He always left just enough for plausible deniability, so it was very rare you could 100% blame him. But every time, you knew …"

After securing his 2015 title, Hamilton appeared to take his eye off the ball and Rosberg went on a seven-race winning spree, claiming the last three races of 2015 and the first four of 2016 to give himself a realistic chance of finally overcoming his nemesis. But tensions boiled over at the Spanish Grand Prix, at which Rosberg arrived with a 43-point championship lead.

Hamilton took pole but Rosberg went around the outside of Turn 1 before losing a bit of power when, due to a mistake he'd made on the formation lap, Nico found himself in the wrong engine mode. Lewis got a better run out of the high-speed Turn 3 right-hander and flicked right in an attempt to go down the inside for Turn 4. Rosberg saw him coming and moved to block him, forcing Hamilton towards the grass. With a lift likely to lose him places he kept his boot in but lost control as he was forced off the circuit and T-boned Nico's car, putting the two Mercedes out on the spot (and handing a first race win to Max Verstappen). Both blamed the other and team principal Toto Wolff had to engage in some emergency diplomacy. Race stewards, meanwhile, assessed it as a racing incident.

Hamilton hit back with his first 2016 victory in round 6 at Monaco and following up with another win in Canada before Rosberg responded by taking the European Grand Prix at Baku. Then came Austria and more controversy.

Rosberg looked to be controlling the race but started to suffer from a long brake pedal in the closing stages and Hamilton closed him down. When Nico missed the Turn 1 apex and ran wide on exit, Hamilton seized his opportunity and went for a pass around the outside of Turn 3. Rosberg, defending, was too late on the brakes, ran straight on, hit Hamilton's car and damaged his own front wing. Hamilton survived the contact and won the race, while Rosberg dropped to fourth while he sorted himself out. An angry Wolff said that they'd risked a double DNF, called the incident "brainless" and threatened the imposition of team orders if they couldn't race cleanly.

Hamilton made it four wins in succession when he won Silverstone, Hungary and Germany, overhauling Rosberg's early-season start and putting himself 19 points clear at the top of the championship table. It looked like a repeat of the familiar story from 2014 and 2015.

But this time Rosberg was made of sterner stuff. He hit back with his own hat-trick of wins at Spa, Monza and Singapore to head the points table again by eight points. The next race in Malaysia was key. Hamilton, dominant all weekend, was leading comfortably when he suffered a blown engine, while Rosberg finished fourth. It was Lewis's fourth non-score of the season for reasons beyond his control and frustrated, he let fly about Mercedes reliability which, in light of the preceding two and a half seasons, did seem a little unreasonable.

What he also left hanging was his belief that there was someone who did not want him to win the championship that year, without making it clear whether he was referring to the good Lord or a faction within Mercedes. "Every remark, every

Opposite Mercedes team principal Toto Wolff was tasked with calming the waters when things overheated between Hamilton and Rosberg, who narrowly won the '16 title after back-to-back championships from Hamilton in 2014–15. Nico then promptly retired.

Above Hamilton and Rosberg splash through the puddles in Hungarian GP qualifying, 2016.

Right Rosberg celebrates victory in the 2016 Belgian GP at Spa.

Below Hamilton leads Rosberg and the field into Turn 1 at the Abu Dhabi championship-decider in 2016.

Opposite Father and son World Champions 34 years apart. Keke Rosberg demonstrates his title-winning Williams FW08 and Nico his Mercedes W07 at Monte Carlo in 2018.

reaction, is allowed after such a frustrating moment," Toto Wolff smiled diplomatically.

When Rosberg won the following race in Suzuka with Hamilton third, Nico had one hand on the championship trophy. With a 33-point advantage, it meant that he could afford to finish second to Hamilton at each of the four remaining races and still take the title by five points.

Which is exactly what happened. Hamilton cleaned up in Austin, Mexico City, Interlagos and Abu Dhabi, with Rosberg second each time. Hamilton made it hard for him at the Abu Dhabi finale, however, moderating his pace in an attempt to back Rosberg into the following pack and force him to watch his mirrors for Sebastian Vettel and Verstappen. Hamilton was harangued by his team from the pit wall and criticized for unsportsmanlike behaviour in some quarters but, realistically, what else was he going to do? Wolff later admitted that it was wrong for the team to interfere, with the Constructors' Championship already in the bag.

It had been a nerve-wracking final race for the delighted Rosberg, who was now part of an exclusive club of just two families who could boast father-and-son World Champions. The Hill family had achieved it when Graham won world titles in 1962 and 1968, with Damon champion in 1996; and now the Rosbergs, with Keke champion in 1982 and Nico 34 years later.

The effort and focus necessary to achieve his ambition had taken its toll on Rosberg and just a few days later, at the FIA's year-end awards ceremony, he made a surprise retirement announcement. He was now the father of a young daughter, wife Vivian was pregnant with their second child and, in his head,

it was the right time. And, just possibly, he might have secretly liked to finish his rivalry with Hamilton on top, without Lewis having the chance to fight back. Like his 2014 Monaco pole.

Hamilton said, "It's the first time he's won in 18 years, so it's not a surprise to me he decided to stop." If that sounded a little disparaging it may not have been meant to, and he added, "He's got family to focus on and F1 takes up so much of your time. I'm going to miss the rivalry because we started karting against each other when we were 13 and when I joined Mercedes, Nico was already there. The sport will miss him and it's going to seem a bit strange without him."

Hamilton, of course, coped just fine, winning the next four championships alongside Rosberg's replacement Valtteri Bottas, to move level with Michael Schumacher on seven world titles, before FIA race officials and a brilliant Max Verstappen decided his reign should end in 2021.

Hamilton vs. Verstappen

Hamilton
103 Grand Prix wins
7 Championships

Verstappen
29 Grand Prix wins
1 Championship

The 2021 season was arguably the most compelling in the 70-year history of the Formula 1 World Championship. It featured intense rivalry between Lewis Hamilton, shooting for a record eighth title, and 23-year-old Dutchman Max Verstappen, already six years into his F1 career and fully ready to claim Hamilton's crown; two of the best drivers ever to pilot a grand prix car backed by two first-class, well-resourced teams in Mercedes and Red Bull.

Verstappen versus Hamilton really was the irresistible force versus the immovable object. From the moment that Hamilton arrived in F1 in 2007 he demonstrated blinding speed, relentless competitiveness and canny judgement in wheel-to-wheel combat. But then, in 2014, along came Verstappen, son of former F1 driver Jos, who made more than 100 race starts and twice stood on the podium. Jos was the Benetton driver engulfed in a fireball that erupted over his car during a pit stop at the German Grand Prix of 1994. At the tender age of 17 years and three days, his son Max became the youngest ever to take part in an F1 race weekend when he drove in the first session of free practice at the 2014 Japanese Grand Prix in preparation for a full season with Toro Rosso in 2015.

Verstappen has impeccable racing genes. As well as Jos, his mum, Belgian Sophie Kumpen, finished ninth in the world karting championship as a 16-year-old. "Sophie was a fantastic driver," Jenson Button revealed. "When I was racing karts in 1995 she was my teammate, so I know how good she was."

Verstappen's God-given talent was obvious the minute he arrived in the sport's top echelon. There were open mouths when he passed Felipe Nasr's Sauber at Spa's flat-out Blanchimont at close to 200mph in his debut season, bouncing over the kerbs but keeping his foot in. Max believed it was possible after doing it while simulated racing!

But he was also causing ructions, both within his own Toro Rosso team, and outside. In Monte Carlo, he took off over the back of Romain Grosjean's Lotus and crashed out. In Singapore, he ignored an instruction from his team to let teammate Carlos Sainz through. But despite the excesses of youth, team principal Franz Tost and Red Bull's Helmut Marko were in no doubt about his talent.

The Red Bull motorsport organization can be a brutal environment and, knowing how ambitious the Verstappens were, and with continued interest from Mercedes boss Toto Wolff, who was in regular contact with Jos, they took the decision to demote Daniil Kvyat and replace him with Max in the senior team in time for the Spanish Grand Prix of 2016. After the Mercedes pair took each other out, Max won on his debut in Barcelona, much to the annoyance of new teammate Daniel Ricciardo, who had been given a different strategy.

Verstappen knew he had the talent and wanted to be competing for race wins and championships. In the senior team, he hoped to do that, but Red Bull wasn't quite there; the frustration started to show and the incidents began to mount. There was a love/hate relationship with Monaco, where Max crashed at the Swimming Pool in 2016 and again in 2018, during practice. At Spa, he deeply upset Kimi Räikkönen with his weaving defence down the Kemmel straight at 200mph. The 'Ice Man' was anything but cool when he yelled, "Hey, come on, this is fucking ridiculous now! He's just f***ing turning as I'm going full speed down the straight!"

At Hungary in 2017, at Turn 2, he thumped the sidepod of teammate Ricciardo, who enquired, "Is that who I think it was? Sore loser …" In Azerbaijan, the two Red Bulls were evenly matched and were running fourth and fifth, Max having just overcut Ricciardo at a tyre stop. As Daniel launched an overtaking move down the main straight into Turn 1, Verstappen moved late and took them both out of the race. Max was clearly at fault but, as Mark Webber found at Turkey 2010, Ricciardo was dismayed to find the management cutting the favoured son some slack and refusing to apportion blame. It was a factor in Ricciardo's decision to move elsewhere for 2019.

Then, famously, there was Brazil in 2018, where Esteban Ocon, on fresh tyres, attempted to unlap himself from Verstappen. Max was leading the grand prix at the time and they made contact. At the end of the race Verstappen, who lost the victory to Lewis Hamilton because of the incident, went to confront Ocon who was waiting to be weighed. After exchanging words with the Frenchman, Max shoved him aggressively a number of times. It was enough to send Verstappen to the stewards and resulted in Max being ordered by the FIA to complete two days of 'public service'.

From the moment Verstappen took pole and won comfortably in the 2020 Abu Dhabi season-closer, both team and driver were optimistic they could mount a serious challenge to Hamilton and Mercedes in 2021. Late regulation changes from the FIA affecting the aerodynamics of the critical rear diffuser hampered the low-rake Mercedes chassis far more than its high-rake Red Bull rival. What's more, the changes came *after* the teams had been asked to submit their Development Tokens, the areas in which they could change the car through the season. The Milton Keynes team commenced the year with the smallest of advantages but a mid-season Mercedes update redressed the balance in Brackley's favour and produced an epic season that went right down to the last lap of the last race in Abu Dhabi. Despite Mercedes looking less than their usual confident selves in pre-season testing, Hamilton narrowly won the Bahrain season-opener on strategy. Verstappen passed him in the closing stages but was judged to have exceeded track limits and had to give the place back.

Right from season's start Verstappen was taking no prisoners. He was tough on the opening lap of the Emilia Romagna Grand Prix at Imola, running Hamilton wide at a chicane and he was aggressive again on the opening lap in Spain, taking the lead at Turn 1 and leaving Hamilton a 'yield or crash' option. Lewis then produced one of his best drives to overhaul Verstappen after Mercedes pitted him twice to take advantage of an extra set of fresh medium-compound Pirellis.

Verstappen hit back with his first victory in Monaco. Baku was also a Red Bull track and Max had the race in the bag when his left-rear Pirelli blew apart with just six laps remaining. Although it looked like terrible misfortune there was a suspicion that some teams were running their tyres lower than the pressures advised by Pirelli. Hamilton failed to capitalize when he accidentally engaged his 'brake magic' button for the restart. Used only on a Formation/Safety Car lap to move the brake bias forward and generate heat in the front tyres, it caused Hamilton to lock up as he braked for Turn 1 and shot down the escape road with his tyres wreathed in smoke – an expensive error and all Lewis's own doing.

Opposite Red Bull teammates Verstappen and Daniel Ricciardo fight in the Azerbaijan GP, 2018. It was a tussle that would end in tears …

Left When F1 returned to the Netherlands and Zandvoort in 2021, for the first time in 36 years, Verstappen delighted his home fans with a consummate win.

Below Verstappen and Hamilton dispute the lead at the '21 US GP at Circuit of the Americas in Austin, Texas.

Above Hamilton tries to go around Verstappen's outside on the opening lap of the '21 Emilia Romagna GP at Imola.

Right Verstappen took half points by 'winning' the race that never was – the shortest in F1 history – at Spa, Belgium, in '21.

Opposite Both Red Bulls were victims of a mistake by Valtteri Bottas in the Mercedes on the opening lap of the '21 Hungarian GP.

Overleaf While Hamilton was penalised for a coming-together with Verstappen at Silverstone, Max was held accountable for this collision at Monza, suffering a three-place grid drop at the next race.

In France, Verstappen and Red Bull won a strategy battle every bit as gripping as Hamilton's Spanish success. It was the first win of a hectic Verstappen triple-header hat-trick, successive victories in two races at Red Bull Ring (previously the Österreichring) in Austria following on at a time of the season when Mercedes and Hamilton were on the back foot. At this point, Verstappen led the championship by 32 points. Just two races later though, that had morphed into an eight-point deficit when Verstappen was taken off on the opening lap by Mercedes drivers at consecutive races.

Silverstone was highly contentious. This was Formula 1's first-ever sprint qualifying event, whereby qualifying was held on Friday before a 100km sprint 'race' on Saturday decided Sunday's grid. While Verstappen was marginally quicker on soft-compound rubber during practice in the heat of the day, the 6pm timing of Friday qualifying suited the Mercedes better and allowed Hamilton to pip Verstappen by 0.07 seconds.

But, in the hotter conditions of the sprint race, the tables were turned, the Red Bull was quicker and Verstappen beat Hamilton to the first sprint win. That was likely to be the competitive picture on Sunday too, so Hamilton knew that unless he could lead the opening lap, Verstappen would be gone.

After Verstappen had been characteristically aggressive to maintain his starting advantage, Hamilton launched a move down the inside of the high-speed Copse corner, clipping the Red Bull's right rear tyre as Verstappen turned in, sending Max to a 51g impact with the tyre wall.

It was Hamilton being opening-lap-tough in the same manner Verstappen had been at Imola and Barcelona; offering Max the same lift-or-crash decision. It's just that Copse, at 180mph, was upping the stakes quite considerably. Hamilton was handed a 10 second penalty that some viewed as harsh and some viewed as ridiculously lenient, but he was still in the race and not on the way to Northampton General Hospital.

At a wet Hungaroring, Hamilton's teammate Valtteri Bottas made a mistake on the brakes into Turn 1 and skated into Lando Norris who, in turn, punted off Verstappen. The restart produced the bizarre sight of Hamilton's Mercedes being the lone car on the grid, on intermediates, as everyone behind him pitted for slicks at the end of the formation lap. He clawed his way back to second place as Fernando Alonso defended, allowing Alpine teammate Esteban Ocon to claim his maiden GP victory. A disgruntled Verstappen, with a badly damaged Red Bull, through absolutely no fault of his own, could only score two points for ninth.

By now the pressure was ramping up and things were getting personal between the rival camps as the legality or otherwise of sundry flexing wings on both cars became a bone of contention. Red Bull team principal Christian Horner said: "With that wing on his car, Toto should keep his mouth shut …" Wolff hit back with, "Christian's a windbag who likes to be in front of the camera." All grist to the mill for Netflix's *Drive to Survive* docuseries which was doing wonders for F1's audience numbers.

Then came a farcical Spa, with points awarded for a race that didn't happen. Torrential rain on race day delayed the start, with the Safety Car pounding around the circuit in vain. The start was delayed beyond two hours, a race most agreed should never have been started, before the cars were brought in from their slow-speed

laps behind the Safety Car. But with Max on pole, he cashed in more points.

The first Dutch GP since 1985 was a triumph for Verstappen, winning assuredly from pole in front of his orange army of fans, despite the huge national weight of expectation on his shoulders. Pressure – what pressure? Then came a second controversial coming-together between the title protagonists at Monza's first chicane.

Verstappen fell behind and tried to run around the outside of Hamilton's Mercedes in Turn 1 before bouncing off the sausage kerb in Turn 2 and coming to rest on top of car No.44, his tyre crushing down on Hamilton's helmet and signalling the end of the race for both. This time blame was apportioned squarely on Max, who was given a three-place grid drop for the following race at Sochi.

Mercedes, by now, had the quicker car with Hamilton winning in Russia and Bottas in Turkey. But Verstappen was able to steady the ship with a mature drive to edge Hamilton by the narrowest of margins at Circuit of the Americas in Texas. He followed up with another win in Mexico, brilliantly taking the lead into Turn 1, deep on the brakes from third on the grid. Horner waxed lyrical: "It's the way that Max extracted the performances … You only have to think of that first turn in Mexico and the Austin race as two examples of him driving out of his skin to keep us in it."

Brilliant races from Verstappen no doubt, but Hamilton matched or even surpassed them with his performance in Brazil. He was booted out of qualifying after Red Bull protested the Mercedes rear wing. It was found to be 0.2mm too wide on one side, an infringement that some found hard to believe that Red Bull could spot. Lewis was forced to start the last of the three experimental sprint races from the back of the grid. After just 24 laps of Interlagos, he was fifth. And, on Sunday, commuted that into one of his greatest victories.

During the course of it, there was controversy as Hamilton tried to go around the outside of Verstappen in Turn 4 and Max ran them both off the track. When the stewards took no action, Mercedes requested a right of review into Verstappen's driving, just as Red Bull had done over Hamilton's at Silverstone, with both denied. However, it left F1 drivers in a total quandary – what was allowable and what was not …?

Lewis now came on strong, comfortably beating Verstappen at a new Losail venue in Qatar. Max finished second after a grid penalty for not respecting waved yellow flags dropped him to seventh on the grid. He went to the penultimate round at the new 155mph average speed Jeddah Corniche street track for the first Saudi Arabian GP, eight points to the good. But pace-wise, Red Bull was now hanging on.

But what followed in the race left a question mark. Verstappen had that eight-point margin and two more race victories to his name. If neither he nor Lewis finished the penultimate round, Max would carry that advantage into Abu Dhabi, where the chance of anyone splitting them was around zero. Cynics would argue that Verstappen tried to end the race early when he jumped on the brake pedal with 69-bar pressure and 2.4g deceleration when told to give Hamilton the place back after running off at Turn 1. And he did it in the middle of the road.

Opposite Max Verstappen heads the field into Sainte Devote on the way to winning the '21 Monaco GP.

Above Hamilton survived a contact when Verstappen suddenly slowed in Saudi Arabia, winning the inaugural GP here and going to the Abu Dhabi decider level on points.

Left A winded Verstappen climbs out after his 51 g impact following a tap by Hamilton at Silverstone's high-speed Copse Corner in '21.

In the Mercedes pit there was fury at the resulting contact but, amazingly, Hamilton did not lose his front wing and he was able to continue at unabated pace, make the pass as Verstappen's less durable medium tyres cried enough, and win the race. The stewards saw fit to add 10 seconds to Verstappen's race time, the effect of which was nothing, so unbelievably they headed to the Abu Dhabi season finale all square. Many thought Max fortunate to avoid a grid drop at the final race, but there were greater twists to come.

A whole book could be written on the shenanigans at Yas Marina Circuit, but with five laps of the race to go Hamilton was leading and on his way to an eighth World Championship, when Nicholas Latifi put his Williams in the wall after running wide at Turn 14.

Out came the Safety Car. Hamilton carried on in front while Verstappen was immediately into the pits for a set of Pirelli soft-compound tyres. Mercedes was backed into a corner. If they'd pitted Hamilton, Verstappen would have stayed out, taken the lead and won the championship behind the Safety Car. It didn't look as if there was sufficient time to restart the race. Article 48.12 of the sporting regulations said: "Once the last lapped car has passed the leader the Safety Car will return to the pits at the end of the FOLLOWING lap. Mercedes concluded they would be home safe.

It took some time to remove Latifi's Williams and sweep away the debris. Initially there was a race control communication stating that lapped cars would not be able to overtake, which is within the race director's powers to decide. With five of them – Lando Norris, Alonso, Ocon, Charles Leclerc and Sebastian Vettel – between Hamilton and Verstappen, it was highly unlikely that Verstappen would get to Hamilton even if the race did recommence. Then Race Director Michael Masi changed his mind and on the penultimate lap, waved through the cars between the two title contenders to unlap themselves … but not the rest.

The Safety Car came in early and gave Max a one-lap shot at overtaking Hamilton on 43-lap-old tyres. Lewis was a sitting duck. Predictably, Max exploited his much superior grip, launched the Red Bull down the inside of Hamilton into Turn 5, weaved to break the tow down to Turn 6, and scampered clear through the twisty final sector of the lap to clinch his first title to great delirium on the Red Bull pit wall.

Mercedes lodged two protests, one against Verstappen for overtaking before the restart, and one against the procedural irregularities of the restart. Both were rejected. Keen not to seem like sore losers Mercedes decided not to take the case to the World Motorsport Council on the understanding that there would be changes in race control.

Over the 22 races Verstappen was a deserving champion having led 652 of the season's laps to Hamilton's 348. But it was a derisory way to end arguably the best season in the championship's history and a terrible way for Lewis, who remained dignified through it all, to lose his crown. An internal FIA investigation was launched and Masi was moved to a new role for 2022 when battle would rejoin. But, in 2022, it would not be Lewis Hamilton and Mercedes challenging Verstappen, but Charles Leclerc and Ferrari.

Index

Page numbers in *italics* refer to illustrations

IVY PRESS

All statistics included in this book are correct as of August 2022.

First published in 2023 by Ivy Press,
an imprint of The Quarto Group.
1 Triptych Place,
London, SE1 9SH,
United Kingdom
T (0)20 7700 6700
www.Quarto.com

A catalogue record for this book is available from the
British Library.

ISBN 978-0-7112-8071-7
Ebook ISBN 978-0-7112-8073-1

10 9 8 7 6 5 4 3 2 1

Design by Glenn Howard
Printed in China

MIX
Paper from
responsible sources
FSC® C016973